Writing and Presenting a Business Plan

Carolyn Boulger Karlson

6 Managerial Communication Series | Editor: James S. O'Rourke, IV

SOUTH-WESTERN
CENGAGE Learning

Australia • Brazil • Japan • Korea • Mexico • Singapore • Spain • United Kingdom • United States

SOUTH-WESTERN
CENGAGE Learning

**Writing and Presenting a Business Plan,
Managerial Communication Series,
2nd edition**

James S. O'Rourke IV, series editor;
Carolyn Boulger Karlson, author

Vice President of Editorial, Business:
Jack W. Calhoun

Vice President/Editor-in-Chief:
Melissa Acuna

Acquisitions Editor: Erin Joyner

Developmental Editor: Daniel Noguera

Marketing Manager: Mike Aliscad

Associate Content Project Manager:
Jana Lewis

Media Editor: John Rich

Managing Media Editor: Pam Wallace

Manufacturing Coordinator: Diane Gibbons

Production Service: Pre-Press PMG

Art Director: Stacy Jenkins Shirley

Internal Designer: Robb & Associates

Cover Designer: Robb & Associates

For product information and technology assistance, contact us at
Cengage Learning Academic Resource Center, 1-800-423-0563

For permission to use material from this text or product,
submit all requests online at **www.cengage.com/permissions**
Further permissions questions can be emailed to
permissionrequest@cengage.com

Library of Congress Control Number: 2008926107

ISBN-13: 978-0-324-58422-6

ISBN-10: 0-324-58422-9

South-Western Cengage Learning
5191 Natorp Boulevard
Mason, OH 45040
USA

Cengage Learning products are represented in Canada by
Nelson Education, Ltd.

For your course and learning solutions, visit **academic.cengage.com**

Purchase any of our products at your local college store or at our
preferred online store **www.ichapters.com**

Printed in Canada
1 2 3 4 5 6 7 11 10 09 08

AUTHOR BIOGRAPHIES

Dr. Karlson is Associate Vice President for Graduate, Weekend, and Accelerated programs at College of Notre Dame of Maryland. From 1996 through 2005, she taught management communication and entrepreneurship courses in the Mendoza College of Business at the University of Notre Dame.

Dr. Karlson serves as an advisor to the Gigot Center for Entrepreneurial Studies, where she mentors finalist teams of undergraduates, graduate students, and Notre Dame alumni in annual business plan competition events. She has worked as a business reporter and editor for regional and national publications, and in public relations and university development as an editor and grant writer.

She is the author of e-Technology and the Fourth Economy (South-Western College Publishing, 2003), and of the first edition of Writing and Presenting a Business Plan (South-Western College Publishing, 2006). She holds a Mass Media Ph.D. from Michigan State University, a Master of Science in Journalism from Columbia University, and a Bachelor of Arts from Simmons College in Boston.

James S. O'Rourke teaches management and corporate communication at the University of Notre Dame, where he is Founding Director of the Eugene D. Fanning Center for Business Communication and Concurrent Professor of Management. In a career spanning four decades, he has earned an international reputation in business and corporate communication. Business Week magazine has twice named him one of the "outstanding faculty" in Notre Dame's Mendoza College of Business.

His publications include *Management Communication: A Case-Analysis Approach* from Prentice-Hall, now in second edition, and *Business Communication: A Framework for Success* from Thomson Learning. Professor O'Rourke is also senior editor of a seven-book series on Managerial Communication and is principal author or directing editor of more than 100 management and corporate communication case studies.

Professor O'Rourke is a graduate of Notre Dame with advanced degrees from Temple University and the University of New Mexico, and a Ph.D. in Communication from the S. I. Newhouse School of Syracuse University. He has held faculty appointments at the United States Air Force Academy, the Defense Information School, the United States Air War College, and the Communications Institute of Ireland. He was a Gannett Foundation Teaching Fellow at Indiana University in the 1980s, and a graduate student in language and history at Christ's College, Cambridge University in England during the 1970s.

Professor O'Rourke is a member and trustee of the Arthur W. Page Society, and a member of the Reputation Institute and the Management Communication Association. He is also a regular consultant to Fortune 500 and mid-size businesses throughout North America.

TABLE OF CONTENTS

FOREWORD

In recent years, for a variety of reasons, communication has grown increasingly complex. The issues that seemed so straightforward, so simple not long ago are now somehow different, more complicated. Has the process changed? Have the elements of communication or the barriers to success been altered? What's different now? Why has this all gotten more difficult?

Several issues are at work here, not the least of which is pacing. Information, images, events, and human activity all move at a much faster pace than they did just a decade ago. Among the more popular, hip new business magazines in recent years is *Fast Company*. Readers are reminded that it's not just a matter of tempo, but a new way of living we're experiencing.

Technology has changed things, as well. We're now able to communicate with almost anyone, almost anywhere, 24/7 with very little effort and very little professional assistance. It's all possible because of cellular telephone technology, digital imaging, the Internet, fiber optics, global positioning satellites, teleconferencing codecs, high-speed data processing, online data storage and... well, the list goes on and on. What's new this morning will be old hat by lunch.

Culture has intervened in our lives in some important ways. Very few parts of the world are inaccessible any more. Other people's beliefs, practices, perspectives, and possessions are as familiar to us as our own. And for many of us, we're only now coming to grips with the idea that our own beliefs aren't shared by everyone and that culture is hardly value-neutral.

The nature of the world in which we live—one that's wired, connected, mobile, fast-paced, iconically visual, and far less driven by logic—has changed in some not-so-subtle ways in recent days. The organizations that employ us and the businesses that depend on our skills now recognize that communication is at the center of what it means to be successful. And at the heart of what it means to be human.

To operate profitably means that business must now conduct itself in responsible ways, keenly attuned to the needs and interests of its stakeholders. And, more than ever, the communication skills and capabilities we bring to the workplace are essential to our success, both at the individual and at the societal level.

So, what does that mean to you as a prospective manager or executive-in-training? For one thing, it means that communication will involve more than simple writing, speaking, and listening skills. It will involve new contexts, new applications, and new technologies. Much of what will affect the balance of your lives has yet to be invented. But when it is, you'll have to learn to live with it and make it work on your behalf.

The book you've just opened is the sixth in a series of seven that will help you to do all of those things and more. It's direct, simple, and very compact. The aim of my colleague Professor Carolyn Boulger Karlson of Notre Dame is not to provide you with a broad-based education in either business or communication, but rather to explore the process of communication and entrepreneurship in *Writing and Presenting a Business Plan*. In a step-by-step approach, she takes us from good ideas ("remember, an idea is not a business, it's just an idea") through feasibility analysis, to a fully developed business plan. She explains how to identify and influence sources of funding for a new venture, how to package your ideas for the marketplace, and how to present your plan to a venture capitalist. Detailed formats and complete business plans are included.

In the first volume of the series, Professor Bonnie Yarbrough focuses on communication issues associated with *Leading Groups and Teams*. Her approach draws on both time-honored principles as well as the latest research in group dynamics and demonstrates why team communication may be among the more important yet least understood communication issues for managers.

In this series' second volume, Professors Robert Sedlack of Notre Dame, Barbara Shwom of Northwestern University, and Chicago management consultant Karl Keller focus on *Graphics and Visual Communication for Managers*. They'll show you subtle differences in typeface, font size, page layout, and document design, as well as help you develop skills in color appreciation, screening, cropping, graph design, and the effective use of PowerPoint to make you more capable as a business communicator.

In volume three, Professor Sandra Collins of the University of Notre Dame explains the process involved in *Managing Conflict and Workplace Relationships*. The conceptual framework she offers involves far more than dispute resolution or determining how limited resources can be allocated equitably among people who think they all deserve more. She shows us how to manage our own emotions, as well as those of others. Creative conflict, organizational harmony, and synchronicity in the workplace are issues that too many of us have avoided simply because we didn't understand them or didn't know what to say.

In volume four, Professor Elizabeth Tuleja of the Wharton School at the University of Pennsylvania and the Chinese University of Hong Kong, examines *Intercultural Communication for Business*, looking both broadly and specifically at issues and opportunities that will seem increasingly important as the business world shrinks and grows more interdependent. As time zones blur and fewer restrictions are imposed on the global movement of capital, raw materials, finished goods, and human labor, people will cling fiercely to the ways in which they were enculturated as youngsters. Culture will become a defining characteristic, not only of peoples and nations, but of organizations and industries.

Volume five, again by Professor Sandra Collins, explores issues associated with *Interpersonal Communication: Listening and Responding*. Her work draws on the latest findings in behavioral psychology and demonstrates why listening and personal interaction may be among the most important yet underdeveloped skills we possess. Becoming an active interpersonal communicator, tuning in to the emotional as well as cognitive content of what we hear, and learning to provide timely, targeted, and meaningful responses are among the most important things we can do for our customers, employees, coworkers, shareholders, and others we deal with in the workplace each day.

In volume seven, Professor Sandra Collins explores the processes at work in *Persuasion*. Her approach is at once theoretical and practical, as she takes you through the latest research findings in behavioral psychology and then shows how they can be applied in workplace settings ranging from corporate offices to sales conferences. Numerous examples and illustrations will help you understand why each of us comes to believe what we do, and how we're each susceptible to influence from others around us. It's a fascinating read and a pragmatic application of both scientific principles and professional best practices.

This is an interesting, exciting, and highly practical series of books. They're small, of course, not intended as comprehensive texts, but as supplemental readings, or as stand-alone volumes for modular courses or seminars. They're engaging because they've been written by people who are smart, passionate about what they do, and more than happy to share what they know. And I've been happy to edit the series, first, because these authors are all friends and colleagues whom I know and have come to trust. Secondly, I've enjoyed the task because this is really interesting stuff. Read on. There is a lot to learn here, new horizons to explore, and new ways to think about human communication.

James S. O'Rourke, IV
The Eugene D. Fanning Center Mendoza College of Business
University of Notre Dame Notre Dame, Indiana

MANAGERIAL COMMUNICATION SERIES
Series Editor: James O'Rourke, IV

The Managerial Communication Series includes 7 Modules covering Leadership, Graphics and Visual Communication, Conflict Management, Intercultural Communication, Interpersonal Communication, Writing and Preparing a Business Plan, and Persuasion. Each module can be used alone or customized with any of our best-selling Business Communication textbooks. You may also combine these modules with others in the series to create a course-specific Managerial Communication text.

MODULE 1: LEADING GROUPS AND TEAMS

ISBN-10: 0-324-58417-2
ISBN-13: 978-0-324-58417-2

Module 1 addresses one of the most important functions a manager performs: putting together effective teams and creating the conditions for their success. This edition describes the major theories of group formation and group functioning, and explains how to create, lead, and manage teams.

MODULE 2: GRAPHICS AND VISUAL COMMUNICATION FOR MANAGERS

ISBN-10: 0-324-58418-0
ISBN-13: 978-0-324-58418-9

Module 2 explains the details involved in crafting graphic images that tell a story clearly, crisply, and with powerful visual impact. Using a step-by-step approach, it demonstrates how to create PowerPoint® files that support and enhance a presentation without dominating or overpowering the content of a talk.

MODULE 3: MANAGING CONFLICT AND WORKPLACE RELATIONSHIPS

ISBN-10: 0-324-58419-9
ISBN-13: 978-0-324-58419-6

Module 3 uses an approach that involves far more than dispute resolution or figuring out how limited resources can be distributed equitably among people who think they all deserve more. Readers will learn how to manage their own emotions, as well as those of others in the workplace.

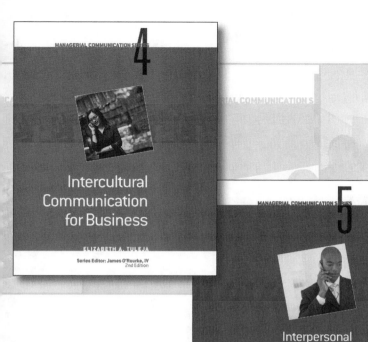

MODULE 6:
WRITING AND PRESENTING A BUSINESS PLAN

ISBN-10: 0-324-58422-9
ISBN-13: 978-0-324-58422-6

Module 6 reviews the entire process of writing and presenting a business plan. From idea generation to feasibility analysis, and from writing the plan to presenting it to various audience groups, this text covers all the steps necessary to develop and start a business.

MODULE 7:
PERSUASION

ISBN-10: 0-324-58421-0
ISBN-13: 978-0-324-58421-9

Module 7 provides a brief overview of both classic and recent social science research in the area of social influence. It offers applications for the business leader for shaping organizational culture, motivating employees, and being an influential manager.

MODULE 4:
INTERCULTURAL COMMUNICATION FOR BUSINESS

ISBN-10: 0-324-58420-2
ISBN-13: 978-0-324-58420-2

Module 4 examines Intercultural Communication for Business, looking both broadly and specifically at issues and opportunities that will seem increasingly important as the business world grows more interdependent.

MODULE 5:
INTERPERSONAL COMMUNICATION: LISTENING AND RESPONDING

ISBN-10: 0-324-58416-4
ISBN-13: 978-0-324-58416-5

Module 5 explores how successful companies and effective managers use listening as a strategic communication tool at all levels of the organization. Common barriers to listening — including culture, perceptions, and personal agendas — are discussed, and strategies for overcoming them are offered.

Contact your local South-Western representative at **800.423.0563**
or visit us online at **academic.cengage.com/bcomm/orourke**.

INTRODUCTION

Perhaps the most important lesson to emerge from the collapse of the dot-com bubble is that entrepreneurs need well thought out, sustainable business models. Groceries by e-mail or rain gear for pets via the Internet somehow never caught on. No matter how interesting the entrepreneurial concept, without a tight, well-designed business model, the venture is unlikely to gain interest from the investment community. Today, that community is simply much more cautious than it was 10 or 15 years ago. They now know that a poorly designed model rarely yields the anticipated performance outcomes. The financial community will simply not consider a venture that does not have a strong business model reflected in a well-written business plan.

Cynics have said that an entrepreneurial vision that cannot be executed is a hallucination. They may be right. A thoughtful, well-crafted business plan certainly increases the likelihood that a venture *can* be launched successfully and the resulting business *can* be sustained. As Professor Carolyn Boulger Karlson shows us, the process of writing a business plan forces the entrepreneur to systematically think about the critical elements of a robust business model in a logical, comprehensive manner. A good business plan communicates the elements of the business model so that the vision, strategy, and tactics of the entrepreneur become clear to the investor and business partner.

Simply put: a good business plan is a living document that evolves with a dynamically competitive business environment. Such plans are really a snapshot, a point in time in the life of a business. Rationally comprehensive, long-term planning is a thing of the past. Dynamism and change are today's business reality. Entrepreneurs are change agents in an economy because they find and exploit opportunities missed by others. And it is the well-crafted business plan that helps an entrepreneur to manage the risks associated with launching a new venture in an environment hostile toward new ideas and change of any sort.

An entrepreneurial business plan is more than a road map. It's a sales document. Its purpose is to sell a vision. It supports a business concept with reliable data and estimations. It demonstrates how the market will accept the product or service, that the market is large enough to merit the business and that the concept is scalable. It also describes the business' revenue model and explains just how its founders, employees, and investors can expect a fair return on their investment. Finally, it provides milestones and financial plans necessary for launching the business.

Professor Karlson's book, *Writing and Presenting a Business Plan*, masterfully describes how an entrepreneurial plan must be written and communicated for a successful venture. She has worked closely with entrepreneurs, investment angels, and venture capitalists for many years. Over the years, Professor Karlson has mentored a number of successful start-ups through the planning and investment process. She has both a keen understanding of the elements of a business model the investment community requires, as well as the concrete business plan they demand. She has eloquently captured both in this book. Entrepreneurs will appreciate the clear and practical way in which she describes the planning process.

Professor Karlson taught Management Communication with distinction at the University of Notre Dame for many years. This book reflects her experience and skill in communicating business ideas: to students, to academics, to investors, to entrepreneurs, and to venture capitalists. Entrepreneurs may have revolutionary ideas—ideas with the potential to transform economies—but if they are unable to communicate those ideas, they'll never see the light of day. Professor Karlson shows readers how to compose, organize, and present those ideas. Her background in communication, journalism, and economics clearly helps her demonstrate the best practices in business plan communication and design.

A Google search of "business-plan guides" will yield more than 22 million hits. Although there is no shortage of business planning tools on the market today, this book is unquestionably among the very best. Read on. Let Carolyn Boulger Karlson show you how you can realize your entrepreneurial dreams.

James H. Davis
Associate Professor of Management
Director, Gigot Center for Entrepreneurial Studies
Mendoza College of Business
University of Notre Dame

1 WHO DO YOU WANT TO BE?

It doesn't matter who you are, where you come from.
The ability to triumph begins with you. Always.

—Oprah Winfrey

Look at these names.

Henry Ford. Bill Gates. Ray Kroc. Michael Dell. Oprah Winfrey. Walt Disney. Mary Kay. Warren Buffet. Donald Trump. Estee Lauder. Jeff Bezos. Steve Jobs. Sam Walton.

Now look at these names.

Deborah Stallings. Brian Mullally. Daniela Papi. Bryan Canepeel. Billy Boniface. Jeff Bernel. Trent Rock. Colin Strutz. Xavier Helgeson. Christopher Fuchs. Josh Francis. Pablo Nava.

What do these two lists have in common? The first group has acclaimed household name status, whereas the latter are virtual unknowns outside of their own households. But they have much in common in that they all took a great idea, a look in the mirror, and a leap of faith to become entrepreneurs. They were ordinary people who became extraordinary by following their entrepreneurial dreams.

It's your turn. Who do you want to be?

Here's the bad news: No one is born an entrepreneur. It's true that such a thing as an "entrepreneurial spirit" exists within those who pursue dreams of creating their own businesses, but entrepreneurship is not the private domain of those who possess that spirit. What's unfortunate is that many people don't believe they could ever do something as daring and risky as starting their own business, even though they probably could if they put their mind to it. Instead, they often select a reason or two from the Letterman-like "Top 10 List of Reasons Why I Can't Start My Own Business."

They are

10. I don't have a college degree.

9. I don't have any money.

8. I think capitalism is the root of all evil.

7. I can't do this by myself.

6. I don't have time.

5. I have a family to support.

4. I am too young.

3. I am too old.

2. More than 75 percent of new businesses fail.

1. Everyone thinks my idea is crazy.

Here's the good news: Anyone can become an entrepreneur. This assumes that your personality include several basic yet often intangible characteristics—an open mind, a positive attitude and strong work ethic, a willingness to accept ambiguity, and an ability to believe in yourself, even when no one else does.

This book will help you tear up the "Top Ten" list and add your name to the much more impressive list of names that lead off this chapter and book. Not convinced? Let Deborah Stallings' story help begin to put your doubts to rest.

NUMBER TEN—"I DON'T HAVE A COLLEGE DEGREE."

It was 1967, and Deborah Stallings was just eight years old and picking cotton on the family farm in Liberty, Mississippi. A little less than 20 years later—inspired by her grandfather who encouraged her to become an entrepreneur, and a grandmother that worked as a midwife and a seamstress—Deborah moved to Maryland and started along a 10-year path that eventually led to her founding her own human resources firm, HR Anew, Inc. The company provides recruiting, employee training, certification and compliance, as well as other human resource work, and brings in more than $1.2 million in revenue a year. HR Anew manages multimillion-dollar contracts for clients such as NASA, the Maryland Transportation Authority, the National Institutes of Health, the Federal Election Commission, the National Library of Medicine, and the Environmental Protection Agency, among others. Her success has not gone unnoticed.

Deborah was named the 2007 Woman of the Year by the National Association of Women Business Owners and the 2007 Women in Business Champion by the U.S. Small Business Administration. She also was honored at the 2007 Maryland's Top 100 Women and the 2006 Maryland Top 100 Minority Business Owners annual competitions.

When she looks back on her success, Deborah says that she didn't pick human resources—human resources picked her. "I moved through my career by getting a call from someone who knew my work—do a good job and people notice," says Deborah. But only when her daughter was safely tucked in college on a full athletic scholarship did she decide to finally strike out on her own.

"The fear of not being successful was always in my mind, but fear stops people from pursuing their dreams," she says. "Internal challenges and emotions will keep you from moving forward if you let them. So I had to keep asking myself, 'what's the worse thing that could happen?' If I failed I wasn't going to become homeless—I could always find another job working for someone else."

Deborah cautions that even when you reach your initial entrepreneurial goals, there's a whole new set of fears waiting for you to conquer. "I know now that I can take care of me with this business, but now I also have 25 employees and 30 to 40 external consultants to provide for. Sometimes that can be a bit scary."

What Deborah has learned to cope and grow through her business transitions is to rely on the power of partnerships and mentors. "No one gets to where they are in life alone," she explains. "I have a humble spirit—I'm always looking to other people to learn from them. I love listening to and learning from people who have walked before me. I pick brains, ask questions, do research, read, attend seminars and workshops, and worship with my community at church. All these things have helped me understand that no one can make it alone. The village sets the stage, and then it's up to the individual to pick up the baton and move forward."

Deborah is now pursuing her Bachelor of Arts degree at College of Notre Dame of Maryland and expects to graduate with the Class of 2010. Incidentally, Oprah Winfrey also grew up on a farm in Mississippi. And Henry Ford didn't have a college degree.

This book is aimed at people like Deborah who hope to proactively improve the odds for long-term success though intensive focus on the steps involved in (1) developing a business idea, (2) conducting a feasibility study, (3) writing a business plan, and (4) presenting that plan to multiple audience groups. Each of the five chapters in this book tackles one of these challenges, featuring interviews with entrepreneurs and numerous examples of what really works at each stage of this process. Each chapter you'll meet two entrepreneurs who each will dispel at least one myth off the "Top 10 List of Reasons Why I Can't Start My Own Business."

This first chapter is devoted to the most instrumental elements of your potential success—your attitudes, expectations, experiences, and assumptions. And of course, your really good idea for a business (you probably wouldn't have picked up this book if you didn't already have one). Consider the following questions as you begin to determine if entrepreneurship is the path for you.

1. How do you handle change and risk? Is it important for you to be able to plan and execute activities without incident? How spontaneous are you? Is it essential for you to set and meet the same goals, or do you adapt goals as situations change?

2. If money were no object, what activities and accomplishments would make you the happiest and most proud? If you were to write your own obituary, what would you want it to say?

3. What life experiences—personal, professional, educational, spiritual, and emotional—have provided the most satisfaction and "sense of peace" so far in your life? List five in each category, and then pick one from each category and rank their impact on your perspective of life.

4. How important are control and routine to you? How important is the end versus the means? How necessary is it for you to control the elements that affect your daily, weekly, and monthly schedules? Your income? Your time away from work?

5. How well do you handle criticism? How have you reacted to past perceived failures? How do you define success?

In general, entrepreneurs see and think past themselves and the present, envisioning possibilities well into the future. But don't let the daydreams fool you—entrepreneurship is by its nature risky and spontaneous. You'll need to adapt to situations for which you may not have fully planned, and you certainly will be asked to multitask. The hours are notoriously long, and there are no guarantees. Begin with the end in mind, but know that you may not realize that end for years if at all, so you need to enjoy the process of building your business, not just its success. That said, do not become paralyzed by the possibility of failure. To be successful, you'll be required to learn from your mistakes and move forward, putting that experience to good use.

So besides thinking about who you want to be as an entrepreneur, it makes a lot of sense to ask what is important to you. Cashing a paycheck should not be your first answer here. Why do you want to do what you want to do, how do your want to do it differently and better than someone else, and where do you think all this could lead? As you begin to answer those questions you formulate the foundation for your business's mission and vision statement. Those answers, combined with knowing what product or service you have to offer and whether the marketplace really wants that product or service at this time, are a perfect start to this process.

It may seem obvious, but you also need to have basic skills in the business areas you hope to enter. It simply doesn't work to solve your lack of relative and crucial experience by hiring the skill sets of others; you must possess them yourself to be credible with both investors and customers. It's fine to outsource services such as legal guidance, tax assistance, and accounting requirements, but it's best to possess the core competencies for which you expect compensation from your customers. This also is invaluable in identifying business opportunities disguised as problems to the untrained eye.

Let's talk ideas. Everyone has them, and everyone thinks that the ones they have are great. Problem is that the eye of the beholder isn't a strong enough litmus test when it comes to ideas for start-up businesses. Also, your first idea may not be your best one, but one that morphs into something better while working through the process of writing a business plan. Much like the novelist who doesn't necessarily know when a plot will twist or a character will mysteriously vanish, the entrepreneur can use the writing process to uncover previously unseen angles and aspects of an idea. That said, not all good ideas make for good businesses, and not all good businesses are good choices for you, given your areas of expertise and experience. Understanding the mechanics of writing and presenting a business plan is not enough to succeed as an entrepreneur—success largely begins with the quality of the idea and the availability of market(s) to support it.

WHAT A GREAT IDEA!

Ideas may appear spontaneous and arbitrary, and indeed sometimes they are so. What may surprise you to know is that you can train yourself to become more prolific in idea generation, just by understanding how they categorize themselves. Good ideas truly are everywhere—you only need the appropriate lens to recognize them when you see them. Through the eyes of an entrepreneur, problems present opportunities for new businesses. Presented next are eight options for generating vibrant ideas for new ventures. Combining these options also presents unique potential for generating numerous ideas for new businesses.

OPTION 1: USE THE PROBLEM/SOLUTION MODEL

Successful start-ups aren't accidental, but certainly, accidents can lead to successful start-ups. Many businesses begin out of frustration as the entrepreneur struggles to solve a problem or fulfill a need. Consider the story of 3M™. Founded in 1902 as a mining company, 3M has spent more than 100 years building successes out of short-term failures. The company was conceived to mine mineral deposits to create grinding-wheel abrasives. Lack of success in this venture prompted the five founders to refocus on a related product, sandpaper. Even then, it took years for the company to determine the appropriate balance between production and supply. Eventually, 3M evolved to become the creator of adhesives such as Scotch® tape, Scotchlite™ Reflective Sheeting for highway markings, magnetic sound recording tape, and Scotchgard™ Fabric Protector, to name only a few products of this now highly diverse and multibillion-dollar company. One of its more notable accidents occurred during the 1980s, when a 3M scientist used an adhesive that didn't stick to create "temporarily permanent" book markers—and a whole new product category—Post-it® Notes.[1]

OPTION 2: APPLY TIME/MONEY FILTERS TO THE PROBLEM/SOLUTION MODEL

What's bothering you today? What took too much time or cost too much money to complete? Or conversely, what didn't take enough time, or cost enough money (yes, that's a legitimate question). Time and money are two of our scarcest resources, with trade-offs between the two a common justification for many business models. How often do you spend $4.65 for a latte while the coffee pot sits half-full at home? In examining your daily habits, which tasks could be made faster or less expensive? Should any become slower and more expensive? Imagine the massage that lasts only 10 minutes—a disappointment for some but for harried airline travelers a welcomed, albeit brief, respite. The entire concept of day spas in airports speaks to the phenomenon of combining two traditionally opposite paradigms of time—the presumption that the pampering of a spa service requires 60 to 90 minutes, or about the time it takes to fly from New York to Chicago.

OPTION 3: GO FOR EFFICIENCY

Creating structure in previously fragmented (but somehow related) markets offers great potential for business ideas. By organizing the disorganized, your business makes life easier and more convenient for both product and service end users as well as for providers and suppliers. The structure and organization offered by your business also may consolidate previously disjointed markets, allowing for reduced duplication of services and costs.

But structure isn't the only option for the efficiency idea model. Efficiency implies that somehow, someway, a situation can be improved upon without starting from scratch. In assessing any situation efficiency aficionados will insert the following words to the statement: "How can I….convert, reduce, enlarge, minimize, maximize, allocate, conserve, distribute, collect, centralize or decentralize this product or service to make it better?" For example, minimizing the ever-shrinking microchip so more information can be stored and displayed in a smaller area makes this option not only extremely efficient but highly marketable. Decentralizing monopolies can create more competition within a marketplace, often driving down price. And reducing…

OPTION 4: SAVE THE WORLD, OR AT LEAST HELP IT OUT A BIT

The United States already has more than 1.4 million not-for-profit organizations, and approximately 47,000 new ones are created each year. The nonprofit sector employs nearly 10 percent of the U.S. workforce.[2] Although starting a nonprofit organization is beyond the scope of this text, "social entrepreneurship," or developing a business that serves the needs of this ever growing market, certainly is a viable option to consider.

OPTION 5: LEVERAGE KNOCKOFFS WITH A TWIST

Starbucks did not invent cappuccino, and Southwest Airlines did not invent air travel, but both companies certainly have left major marks on their respective industries. Each reversed the previous norm of its industry—Starbucks by customizing and up-pricing the cost of a cup of coffee, and Southwest Airlines by eliminating seat assignments and dropping ticket prices. In their unique ways, Starbucks and Southwest Airlines demonstrate that variations on existing business models can prove successful. The lesson here: Don't build from scratch what you can borrow or adapt.

That's essentially what eBay did when it launched an online auction company in 1995. eBay's global trading platform combined the excitement of an auction with the simplicity of a garage sale. eBay created an opportunity for virtually anyone with a computer and Internet access to market or purchase a widely diverse selection of goods and services. The upgrading of the age-old auction model eliminated the need for buyers and sellers to be co-located and created new business opportunities for millions of start-up ventures around the world.[3]

In a similar fashion, the founder of Federal Express challenged previous assumptions of the amount of time it took to transfer items from place to place. In 1965, Yale University undergraduate Frederick W. Smith wrote a term paper about the passenger route systems used by most airfreight shippers, which he viewed as economically inadequate. Smith wrote of the need for shippers to have a system designed specifically for airfreight that could accommodate time-sensitive shipments such as medicines, computer parts, and electronics.[4] The company incorporated in June 1971, began operations in 1973, and became profitable by 1975. Throughout its existence, FedEx has amassed an impressive list of firsts, most notably for leading the industry in introducing new services for customers. FedEx originated the overnight letter and was the first transportation company dedicated to overnight package delivery with guaranteed delivery times.

OPTION 6: PLAY AT WORK

Entertainment is big business. Musicians, writers, and artists have acted as their own CEOs for centuries, searching out markets for their talents and skills. Avid equestrians or skiers may want to share their expertise by opening a tack shop, a sporting goods store, or perhaps even a riding stable or mountain resort. Successful companies such as LEGO and Toys "R" Us (see the mission statements for these companies later in this chapter) are two examples of highly successful businesses with a focus on fun, the former with a focus on a core product with immense popularity, and the latter as one of the world's most visible toy and game distributors.

OPTION 7: SELL YOURSELF

Accountants, lawyers, physicians, dentists, and consultants, to name a few, often opt to be their own bosses rather than join larger firms. They often hire other professionals to complement their services, as well as paraprofessional office support staff. The Small Business Administration labels these entities "small businesses" until they reach the cutoff point of 500 employees. That's a lot of room for you and your business to grow, and an option that many baby boomers are investigating as they migrate toward a "retirement career." Or, like Deborah Stallings, maybe you are now in a position in your personal life to take a chance on your professional one. "Once my daughter had been accepted to college on a full athletic scholarship, I didn't have to worry as much anymore about the implication of my business decision on her future," explains Deborah. "If I had failed, it was only me who I had to worry about."

OPTION 8: CREATE A NEW INDUSTRY

For the true visionary, the opportunity to create not only a business but an entire industry may be the ultimate challenge. Yet even industries we take for granted today had humble beginnings. Walt Disney and his brother, Roy, spent five years getting their start-up studio off the ground before Mickey Mouse was "born" in 1928. Henry Ford and his 11 business associates launched their automobile empire with $28,000. Sam Walton opened with a single store in 1962. They, like you, began with a dream.

In tandem with these options, you'll need to give serious thought at this stage to your potential customers. Who are they? At this stage, you need to answer the most basic of questions: Will they care about your new product or service, and why? What problem does it solve? How will your business make their lives easier, more pleasurable, less painful, or more productive? Never assume that the day you open your doors for business, the customers will automatically appear.

DEFINING YOUR MISSION, VALUES, AND GOALS

The best ideas in the world will remain little more than that if they are not put on paper and transferred into concrete objectives with deliverables and deadlines. The writing process will allow you to objectively view your business as you'll gather information to complete requirements and meet expectations for each business plan section. This task is not a linear writing assignment; you will likely find yourself jumping from section to section as the data-gathering process proceeds. Changes in one section will also trigger changes in others because competition, market share, audience preferences, financial forecasts, and product availability are all interrelated and codependent.

Three sure ways to jump-start the business plan writing process are to prepare first drafts of mission/message statements, a "best scenario" executive summary, and a logo, trademark, or other form of brand identity. Completion of these three components helps the business seem more real by providing early momentum in key business areas.

TASK 1: MISSION/MESSAGE STATEMENTS

Many business plan guides suggest beginning the writing process by developing a *mission statement*, although a mission statement is difficult to write well. A mission statement is a concise paragraph that defines a company's values, goals, and objectives. Mission statements are written to answer four basic questions: (1) why you are in business, (2) how you will succeed, (3) what your product or service is, and (4) who your customers are. Clear and compelling are the goals here, so use direct language and strong verbs in the active voice and present tense.

As you begin writing a draft of your mission statement, be sure to include all aspects that you consider essential: values, goals, customers, and products or services. You may need to write long passages before you can synthesize your thoughts into a short (fewer than 40 words), compelling message. Some companies opt to write several mission statements, each dedicated to a core element of the business. Others include a vision statement, which redefines the future based upon the perceived impact of the new business on its industry.

Reviewing competitors' mission statements in your industry area is a good place to begin; these statements are often found on the companies' Web sites.

TASK 2: BEST SCENARIO EXECUTIVE SUMMARY

An executive summary provides a snapshot of the major components of your business. Generally less than 500 words, summaries include concise yet specific paragraphs explaining your company's history and management, product or service, industry and competition, and market(s) and financial expectations. Your mission/message statement also is included in this document, usually as an introductory paragraph. You'll also want to write a brief description of your management team, highlighting core competencies of each member.

The "best scenario" approach allows you a chance to define your best chance for success in your summary. You will have an opportunity to examine worst-case scenarios as part of the feasibility study process—this is the time to stay positive and idealistic. Most likely you won't have enough information to complete many of the summary categories at this point, but that's acceptable at this stage. You are discovering through this process what you need to find out to eventually make each section as complete as possible. By writing an executive summary now, you can more concretely visualize the work ahead.

TASK 3: CREATE YOUR IDENTITY

You might think the easy part is naming your company. Not so. Selecting a name requires lots of research and anticipation of how you want your customers to identify your brands and services. Here's a list of important considerations to keep in mind when selecting a name for your company.

1. Is it memorable? Will your customers associate your company's name with the products or services offered? For example, many people opt to use their family name as a company name, but without a previous reputation in a given market, there may be no fixed association between your name and those products and services.

2. Is the name of your business difficult to spell or pronounce? Some family names present spelling challenges, potentially making it difficult for customers to find your business through telephone or Web directories. Pronunciation hurdles may impede the word-of-mouth factor that so many new businesses rely on for market growth, because customers may not want to share information about a company if they feel unsure about how to correctly pronounce its name.

3. Are there other businesses in your industry or geographic market that already have laid claim to the name? You'll also need to ask and answer this question as it pertains to a logo for your company and brand identification for all your products and services. In a nutshell, you need to be aware of the federal levels of protection applied to names and other identifying marks "fixed in tangible medium of expression"[5] by those who have established businesses before you. Generally speaking, trademark law protects product names, service marks, logotypes, and slogans. Copyright law protects works fixed in tangible form, such as writings, art, music, movies, and sculpture. Patent law protects inventions and the process you use to create products.

4. Is a Web domain name available that closely matches your company's proposed name? If your company's marketing and sales plans involve Internet transactions, it's essential to answer this question sooner rather than later. To do so, visit a domain registration site such as http://www. register.com and enter the potential names for your business. The site search engine will not only tell you if your desired name is taken, but also provide contact information for who owns it, allowing you the option to privately negotiate for that domain name if you wish. You also will learn what other names are available similar to the one(s) you proposed. Most businesses use a .com extension to indicate their commercial status, but .net and .biz extensions also are options.[6] Some businesses will purchase all available extensions and logical name variations at this stage to allow for redirection of Web traffic to their sites and to ensure that a future competitor won't enter the Web market using a similar domain name.

5. Does your proposed company name have visual potential? Market success is crucial for any business, but perhaps no more so than in the early stages of the company, when brand identification is being cultivated. How will the name you've selected translate to a visual identifier that your customers can instantly identify and relate to? Consider the McDonald's golden arched "M" or the blue, bold blocked "Dell," and you'll begin to recognize the impact of this relationship.

Finally, keep in mind that even the best names of businesses and their products and services are often changed as they evolve through the development process. Investors commonly rename companies as partial conditions for funding, and your feasibility study may determine that the name(s) you've selected aren't adequate to grow with the potential for your business. That's okay—business plan writing is not a linear process. Just do the best you can at this early stage, and have faith that the process outlined in the next four chapters will bring forth many of the answers sought in these preliminary stages of business development.

NUMBER NINE—"I DON'T HAVE ANY MONEY"

It was July 2006 when Brian Mullally heard the words "It can't be done." Most people turn on their heels and scatter when given that assessment from people who should know, but not entrepreneurs, not Brian. Just one year later and with $1.5 million in hand, Brian launched GlobeFunder, the world's first company to offer global peer-to-peer and institutional direct-to-consumer online lending. He raised that money from his friends and family—convincing them one by one that there was nothing small beans about the micro-lending business. He now is halfway toward a new goal of obtaining $6 million through negotiations with venture capitalists. He has accomplished all of this in the span of less time than it takes an elephant to give birth.

What is GlobeFunder? Think eBay for small loans—offering lenders high returns (10 percent to 25 percent), driving down the cost of capital for borrowers (e.g., reducing rates on credit cards by providing debt consolidation at a more attractive rate), and offering institutions an alternative debt market from which they can diversify their portfolios. Their market is the $800 billion U.S. unsecured consumer loan industry, as well as individuals in international markets who need access to cash to launch or grow their own small businesses. To make this work, Bryan and his partners must identify other potential partners in countries they hope to enter and those countries have to be large enough to offer a baseline of potential lenders and borrowers, and have regulatory requirements that permit micro-lending.

"I need to ask and answer—who is there in that country, who can help us? We need concrete relationships in place," explains Bryan. "It's awfully hard to manage this type of business in a country with only 3 to 4 million people."

"We're all about connecting people with people. It is so important to build bridges and relationships," he continues. "What we have learned is that the pace of business development increases exponentially if you take on partners."

In developing his business idea, Brian primarily drew from the problem/solution category of great ideas, but dabbled in at least three other idea categories—time, money, efficiency, and to a lesser extent, saving the world. Here's how it works: A typical borrower has revolving credit card debt that they now realize costs maybe anywhere from 15 percent to 23 percent per month in interest. That's a problem. GlobeFunder solves that problem for borrowers with good credit scores by consolidating that debt, decreasing monthly payments, and lowering interest rates. It does this by matching lenders with borrowers to provide competitive interest rates and lower borrowing costs. That's efficient. It's also a good example of the money option applied to multiple audience groups. When the borrower is a single mother in India hoping to start her own business, Bryan feels that his company helps empower the entrepreneurial spirit by providing access to funds that previously did not exist.

"We answer the question: How can individuals make a major impact on a global scale, and also make it profitable for themselves?" explains Bryan. "Our business provides donors with the type of scale and scope that can really make an impact with international micro-lending."

REVIEW

This is the time when all things are possible. But the only way a business will grow from this dream stage is for you to begin to capture your best thoughts on paper. From there, a feasibility analysis (detailed in Chapter 2) will help you determine your best approach to moving your business forward.

Five key points to remember:

1. Investors aren't sitting around waiting for you to finish your business plan. In most cases, you'll need to invest thousands of your own hours and dollars to prove your concept is viable before outside sources of funding become an option.

2. Working for yourself doesn't mean you work without experience. In fact, exactly the opposite is necessary for success. Start learning about every aspect of your business, and never stop.

3. Now is the time to think big—you can always downsize later. Trying out different options to generate a variety of ideas can only help you at this stage.

4. Low barriers to entry mean high potential for duplication. If anyone could do what you've proposed in your business idea, then why do they need you to do it for them?

5. Start today. Get your dreams for your business out of your head, and put them on paper. Write mission and vision statements, executive summaries, and slogans. Visualize as many aspects of your business as possible, and then fix them in tangible form. Only then will they begin to become real.

ASSIGNMENTS

1. There is no better time than the early stages of business plan development to create a word brainstorm list for your business. Without consideration for whether these labels apply to your company's name, brand, or mission statement, list at least 50 words that you'd like to be affiliated with your business, product, and/or service in some capacity. These can be product-specific words such as *turbo-charged* or goal-oriented words such as *triumph.* Try to avoid mundane adjectives such as *value, quality,* and *best* because their vague nature can trigger subjective interpretations. Your best choices are strong verbs and nouns that have high potential for visualization. Once you've written a master list, you can subcategorize these words according to how they relate to your company today and where you see it evolving in the future. Ultimately, this list will provide a pool of descriptors to draw from as you write your mission statement and other preliminary documents for your company.

2. Write drafts of the mission and vision statements for your business. This is your ultimate mission and vision—not only what you hope to accomplish in the next six months (we'll tackle that challenge when we talk about milestones in Chapter 3).

3. Write a best scenario executive summary. Even if the information needed to complete this task seems highly surreal at this stage, be sure to write something related to all sections of your future business plan. Think big—you're still in the anything-goes land of the hypothetical. Don't skip any key sections because you don't know how to answer them yet. Just fill in what seems right to you at this time.

4. Begin to make your business real by giving it a name and image. Review the logos and trademarks of your competition, both locally and by product or service item. A Web search is particularly useful for this assignment. Select colors and shapes that symbolize the business as you envision it. Draw key words from your word brainstorm list that epitomize what you want your business to stand for. Draft a slogan.

It is from these early decisions and roots that so much of your future business will evolve, so treat these steps with care.

ENDNOTES

1. "History." Retrieved from http://www.3m.com/about3M/history.
2. "National Center for Charitable Statistics." Retrieved from http://nccsdataweb.urban.org/PubApps/profile1.php?state=US.
3. "About eBay." Retrieved from http://pages.ebay.com/community/aboutebay/index.html.
4. "FedEx History." Retrieved from http://www.fedex.com/us/about/today/history/?link=4.
5. Copyright Act of 1976, Public Law 94–553, U.S. Code 17 §102(a).
6. Generally, .org extensions are reserved for not-for-profit organizations, .edu for education-related affiliations, and .gov and .mil for government- and military-related sites, respectively.

2 FROM IDEAS TO ACTIONS

"An entrepreneur tends to bite off a little more than he can chew hoping he'll quickly learn how to chew it."

—Roy Ash, co-founder of Litton Industries

If only it were so easy to take that great idea and turn it into a viable business overnight. It's not, and for good reason. Not all ideas are good, not all are meant to be businesses, or not all are ready to be businesses at this given time. Before investing substantial time and money in your idea, it's necessary to test it out a bit. Taking the time now to do this can save hundreds of hours and hundreds of thousands of dollars later—please don't skip this step! A feasibility study will help accumulate information for your eventual business plan, so certainly it's not time wasted. Many entrepreneurs significantly revamp the scope and focus of their business through this process. If your "great idea" is untimely, impractical, too expensive, or already someone else's business—wouldn't you prefer to know that sooner rather than later? Take a month or two now to find out. This process also will be helpful to understand and apply as your business evolves and grows. Daniela Pepi knows firsthand how important the ability to pivot your plan can be to the successful growth of a business. Here's her story.

NUMBER EIGHT—"I THINK CAPITALISM IS THE ROOT OF ALL EVIL"

After graduating from the University of Notre Dame in 2000, Daniela Pepi accepted a consulting position at a prominent Chicago firm, where she was employed for two years. "I hated it—I hated working at a desk and on a computer all day," says Daniela. Fed up, she finally quit her job, taught skiing for a year, and then moved to Japan to teach English. Along the way, she led volunteer trips in many places around the world—Nepal, Sri Lanka, Papua New Guinea, the Philippines, to name just a few.

"I had watched my fellow volunteers change from their experiences, become inspired by the people we met—the stories we heard," Daniela explains. "We were no longer tourists, we were making friends. We were changing lives. We were learning. We were living and feeling and understanding a place, rather than just looking at a country through a glass plate. Instead of being at the zoo, we were on safari.

"I knew that I wanted to bike ride across Cambodia, so I decided to raise money and do it," she continues. "Then I decided that this would be a great way to raise money for education."

And raise money she did—more than $100,000 in her first year founding and managing PEPY Tours and the PEPY Ride—for-profit and nonprofit organizations, respectively, that have combined adventure, tourism, volunteerism, and philanthropy in a unique and compelling manner. PEPY Tours serves as the tour operator, managing all that goes into that, hiring guides and renting buses, booking hotels and, if need be, hiring third-party tour operators to manage parts of the trip. The PEPY Ride focuses on the philanthropic work, distributing funds to the most effective groups, developing new projects, and tracking the progress of their efforts. "Part of my concern with philanthropy is lack of integrity over where the funds are going. Rather than raising money to give to other organizations to help in Cambodia, we decided to become our own 503c so we could manage those funds directly."

Investors ask Daniela why people would want to raise money for a trip when they could just write a check instead. "But that's the point—they choose us because they have to raise $500 to go on this trip—that's part of the process," explains Daniela. "Then those people who donated money to them will hear about the success of the trip through the rider, and then those donors become our 'word of mouth' advertising."

Funding from the PEPY Ride has built two schools and supported orphanages and education throughout Cambodia. "An individual on his own or her own can't do the types of things to help the world that we can as a group. After my first international volunteer trip to Nepal I knew this was something that I needed to do more of," says Daniela. "And, not only that, I began to understand how this kind of travel is a key to a peaceful world and an educated population. It is what almost every traveler in their 20s and 30s is looking for when they say 'I don't want to be a tourist. I don't want to do touristy things.' PEPY Tours is what they are looking for."

"The younger the customer, the better, because younger people are more likely to fund-raise than write a check. They also aren't set in their careers and lives yet, so this experience has a greater chance of having a profound impact on the rest of their lives," explains Daniela, who has sidestepped paid advertising campaigns in favor of establishing PEPY Clubs on college campuses, and forming a PEPY alumni association on its Web site, complete with stories of past tour participants.

"I work for a for-profit company that chooses to be a good egg—my company. I want to change the fabric of the marketplace and show that a for-profit company can make a difference. If we're not a for-profit, then we can't prove that it can be done," says Daniela.

PLANNING YOUR FEASIBILITY STUDY

Feasibility studies consist of several distinct content areas. These areas include analyses of the industry and the company, the product and/or service, the competition, the markets you plan to enter and serve, and financial pro forma statements. Questions you need to ask and answer in each of these sections are presented in this chapter, as are suggested sequence orders for writing as well as obstacles to avoid in each section.

SECTION 1: THE INDUSTRY AND COMPANY

The objectives of this section of the feasibility study are to provide an overview of your industry and to describe the start-up and background of your company. To do this, you will need to answer the three categories of questions that follow.[1]

CATEGORY 1
What is the company's background?

a. When and where was the company started? (Include the date and state of incorporation or partnership.)

b. Where is the business located? Why?

c. Have you obtained a patent or trademark for the company's name and/or logo?

d. What is the legal structure of the company (S corporation, C corporation, or limited liability partnership)?

e. How was your venture developed?

f. Why did you go into business? How long did it take?

g. What problems were encountered? How did you overcome them? What were the key milestones?

h. Is your company affected by major economic, social, technological, environmental, or regulatory trends?

CATEGORY 2
Who are the founders and other key people involved?

a. What skills and experiences does each member of the team bring to the business?

b. How much money have you/they invested? How has it been used?

c. What have been your other sources of funding?

CATEGORY 3
What industry are you in?

a. What is the current state of the industry? How big is it in terms of total sales? Profits? Margins?

b. Who are the major industry participants (competitors, suppliers, major customers, distributors, etc.)? What is their performance? Market share? What advantages do you have over them?

c. What are the industry's chief characteristics?

d. Where is the industry expected to be in five years? Ten years?

e. Will your share increase or decrease with these changes?

f. Who else may enter the industry?

WRITING YOUR INDUSTRY/COMPANY PROFILE

Your goal in this section is to begin to make the reader a part of your dreams. Describe how your work and decisions got the company where it is. Show how past performance will pave the way to future success. Demonstrate how you will become an important addition to the industry, and show that you understand the industry and where it is headed. You will likely need no fewer than three and no more than five single-spaced typed pages to complete this section of the feasibility study.

The following is a suggested writing sequence for the Industry/Company Profile section of your feasibility study.

Subheadings to include:

The Company

1. Background

2. Current Status

3. Future Plans

The Industry

1. Chief Characteristics

2. Analyst Summaries

3. Trends

THE COMPANY

BACKGROUND

This section allows you to describe the start-up and history of your company from the time of its inception. State what form of business it is and where it is located. Discuss significant milestones, such as obtaining a patent, building a prototype, signing a major contract, or obtaining trademarks on the company's name or logo. Also be sure to discuss critical people involved and the roles they have played so far.

CURRENT STATUS OF COMPANY

Discuss where you are now and how you evolved to this point. Talk about the reputation you have built, your strengths, and any limitations you are experiencing. Describe how your product is performing in the marketplace. State how much money has been invested to date, by whom, and how it has been used. If your business has any sales or service records, highlight them here. Discuss the kind and amount of funding the business needs to begin or improve operations.

FUTURE PLANS OF COMPANY

Outline your professional goals for the next three to five years. Describe how you plan to achieve them and the resources that will be needed. Be sure to allude to improvements and expansion of your existing product line as well as your hopes for increasing your market share and sales.

THE INDUSTRY

CHIEF CHARACTERISTICS OF YOUR INDUSTRY

Describe the industry your company is in by reviewing the industry's size, geographical dispersion, market, history summation, current status, and total sales and profits for each of the past three years. Discuss the competition and other players (suppliers, wholesalers, distributors, etc.) within your industry, offering a summary of each participant from weakest to strongest. Briefly discuss the participants' product/service lines and market niches. Also be sure to discuss participants with whom you will have direct involvement or competition.

ANALYST SUMMARIES OF INDUSTRY

In this section you'll need to provide a series of quotations and statements that summarize significant facts, figures, and trends about the industry from various reputable sources. Be sure you properly credit each source and provide the date of publication. Use quotations and statements from diverse sources such as industry magazines and newspaper articles. Keep in mind that quotations from personal interviews with industry leaders or analysts can also have a powerful impact. These statements should clarify where the industry is headed and the various markets to be served within the industry.

INDUSTRY TRENDS

Based on your research, you should be able to state whether your industry is declining, improving, or maintaining itself. Given your observations, discuss where you predict it might be in five to ten years and how that projection ties into your business plan. To do this, you'll need to discuss the future of the industry in terms of market need and/or acceptance and profit potential, as well as describe significant events or changes within the industry that could affect your business positively or negatively.

WHAT TO WATCH FOR

As you complete this section, you should take care to avoid several common mistakes. One mistake is including too much detail and personal opinion about the company and not enough on significant milestones and potential. Be sure to demonstrate a well-rounded knowledge of major industry players and their potential influence on the company, or you will appear to be a fly-by-night operation evidencing a lack of direction. Finally, be sure to be aware of current industry trends. Demonstrating poor or inadequate knowledge of the industry will raise doubts about the probability of your success in your new venture.

SECTION 2: YOUR PRODUCT AND/OR SERVICE

The primary objectives of this section of the feasibility study are to describe the product and related services, special features, benefits, and future development plans of your company. In three to five pages, explain what is special or different about your product and related services, and describe whom they serve. Also, you'll want to briefly highlight future plans for improvements or for introducing new products and services. To do this, you'll need to answer the following four categories of questions.

CATEGORY 1
What is the purpose of the product and/or service?

a. Does the product solve a problem or address an opportunity?

b. Is it a luxury item/service or a necessary item/service?

c. How does the product/service achieve these objectives?

d. What are its unique features (cost, design, quality, capabilities, etc.)?

e. What is its technological life?

f. What is its susceptibility to obsolescence? To changes in style or fashion?

g. How does it compare with the state of the art?

CATEGORY 2
In what stage of development is the product or service?

a. Idea

b. Model

c. Working prototype

d. Small production runs

e. Manufacturing/production

f. Engineering prototype

g. Production prototype

CATEGORY 3
How will the product be produced?

a. Is it capital intensive? Is it labor intensive? Is it material intensive?

b. Will all or some of the production be subcontracted? Is this an end-use item or a component of another product?

c. Is the product/service dependent on any natural, industry, or market life cycle?

d. Does your company's survival depend on someone else?

e. What new products (spin-offs) do you plan to develop to meet changing market needs, in this industry or others?

f. What liabilities might this product and/or service pose?

g. What are the insurance requirements?

h. What are the regulatory or approval requirements from government agencies or other industry participants?

CATEGORY 4
How does this product/service compare with those of competitors?

a. What kind of engineering studies, testing, and evaluation has the product undergone?

b. If more than one product is involved, how will the manufacture and/or promotion of one affect the other?

c. If equipment is involved, what is its reliability factor? What is its downtime?

d. What are the related services you will provide? How will they enhance and increase the profitability of the venture?

Following is a suggested sequence of presentation for the Product/Service section of your feasibility study.

Subheadings to include:

1. Description of Product/Service

2. Description of the Facilities

3. Proprietary Features

4. Future Development Plans

5. Product Liability

DESCRIPTION OF PRODUCT/SERVICE
Describe exactly what your product/service is, for what purpose it was designed, and what stage of development it is in. Explain in great detail how it works, special features, capabilities, and resulting benefits (economic, social, environmental, leisure, etc.). If more than one service or product is involved, discuss them and how they function together and/or affect each other.

DESCRIPTION OF THE FACILITIES
Like real estate, a major success for any business is location, location, location. Explain why you selected the one you did, referring to other businesses in the area, traffic patterns, and proximity to potential customers. If the facilities are a focus and part of the product or service (such as a hotel would be), describe them in this section. If the design of the business workspace is important to your business's success, describe what makes your facilities unique, better, or more attractive than those of your competitors, and explain why. Include costs per square foot of facilities, and state the percentage of the facilities used for revenue-producing services, operations, storage, and so on.

PROPRIETARY FEATURES

Overall, discuss how you intend to protect the integrity, confidentiality, and competitive nature of your product and service. Briefly mention any regulatory or approval requirements your product or service must meet. State who has jurisdiction and how you will satisfy these requirements. Discuss any patents, copyrights, trademarks, service marks, or other legally binding agreements that protect your product or service. State whether a patent is pending.

FUTURE DEVELOPMENT PLANS

Describe the nature and application of future development plans. Discuss whether these plans are improvements, an extension of the current product/service line, or plans for other products/services. Justify why these plans are important by showing increased or newly generated profits. State whether these plans will address your current market or other markets. Discuss the time frames for accomplishing these plans.

PRODUCT LIABILITY

Discuss the liability and insurance considerations that are inherent in manufacturing and/or marketing the product, and explain how you plan to limit this liability. Explain what type of liability insurance is necessary, and provide an estimate of the percentage of the product's cost that will be applied toward liability coverage.

WHAT TO WATCH FOR

It is extremely important that you fully describe every aspect of your product and/or service. Do not describe the product/service too technically, too broadly, or too ambiguously. Rather, focus on new, unique, or better capabilities, features, or benefits offered by your product/service. As you do this, be sure to consider the reliability, maintenance, and/or updating factors associated with your product or service. Failure to do your homework on protection availability or not showing how to protect the product/service from liability or competition is a serious oversight. Also be sure to write a strong plan for product/service improvements and expansion and how you plan to stay ahead of market needs and competition. Finally, don't forget to obtain at least one third-party evaluation of your product/service—focus group feedback or blind product trials work well here. The best scenario would be to obtain letters of intent to purchase from would-be customers.

SECTION 3: THE COMPETITION

In this section of the feasibility study you'll need to demonstrate that you are fully aware of the competitive forces at work in your marketplace. You'll also need to explain your strengths over the competition and how you will counteract their advantages and overcome or compensate for your weaknesses. Give a brief rundown on the other industry participants, highlighting your particular competitive edge along the way. You will need to answer the following four categories of questions to complete this task.

CATEGORY 1

Who are your nearest and largest major competitors?

a.   Is their business steady, increasing, or decreasing? Why?

b.   What are the similarities or dissimilarities between your business and your competitors?

c. If you have no competition, what kind might you create by being successful in the marketplace?

d. Do you threaten the major strategic objectives or self-image of the competition?

e. Will you seriously affect competitors' profits?

CATEGORY 2
How does your business compare with your competitors' (strengths and weaknesses of each)?

a. Length of time in business?

b. Sales volume (units and dollars)?

c. Size and number of employees, suppliers, and support personnel?

d. Number of customers?

e. Share of market?

f. Product niche?

CATEGORY 3
On what basis will you compete?

a. Product superiority

b. Price

c. Advertising

d. Technology/innovation

CATEGORY 4
How is your business better?

a. Operations

b. Management

c. Product

d. Price

e. Service

f. Delivery

Following is a suggested writing sequence for the Competitive Analysis section of your feasibility study.

Subheadings to include:

1. Competitors' Profile

2. Product/Service Comparison

3. Market Niche and Share

4. Comparison of Strengths and Weaknesses

COMPETITORS' PROFILE

The more you know about your competition, the better. You'll need to examine both current and potential competitors in your desired marketplace based on the demographics of company size, age, locations, sales volume, management, mode of operation, and other characteristics related to similar products and services you will offer.

PRODUCT/SERVICE COMPARISON

Highlight whatever it is that makes your product/service and company more attractive in the marketplace. To do this, review similarities and differences between your product/service and that of the competition. Also be sure to compare your operations and management style with those of your various competitors.

MARKET NICHE AND SHARE

Describe where the market is headed and how each competitor's niche and share may change over the next three to five years. Discuss the competitors who have come or are coming on strong and are making (or are expected to make) bigger gains in the market. Discuss the particular segments of the market that each of your competitors addresses. State the approximate percentage each of your competitors holds in the market.

Discuss those competitors that hold the large percentages, why they have an edge, your niche in relation to them, and what percentage of the total market your niche has.

COMPARISON OF STRENGTHS AND WEAKNESSES

In this section you'll need a straightforward and honest discussion of your strengths and weaknesses in relation to your major competitors. Compare your business with others in terms of product superiority, price advantages, market advantages (large contracts with customers or suppliers; proximity to the larger market; proximity of labor supplies, raw materials, energy, transportation, land, or other resources), and management strengths and weaknesses (experience and track record, skills, etc.).

WHAT TO WATCH FOR

Certainly, you must identify all known major competitors. Do not underestimate competitive strengths and the potential of others in your industry. Be sure to demonstrate your competitive edge—what makes you different or better. Do not assume that you have no competition—this is rarely the case. That false assumption also can cause you to make two additional serious errors: (1) having no strategy for counteracting current competition or emerging competition and (2) failing to show an awareness of competitors' plans in the market and their business cycles.

SECTION 4: THE MARKET ANALYSIS

The goals of this section of the feasibility study are to demonstrate that you understand the market, that you can penetrate it, and that you are in control of the critical success factors that will enable the company to reach its sales goals. Above all, you need to prove that a market for your product/service exists and that your potential share of that market and the resulting profit projections are realistic.

Citing facts from your research and experiences, explain why and how your company will be successful. After answering the following nine sections of questions, you will need seven to ten single-spaced pages to organize the material for your market analysis.

CATEGORY 1
Who or what is your target market?

a. What is the size of your target market?

b. Can this market be segmented? How (by geography, by industries, or other)?

c. Who are your customers? Are they individuals, companies, or government agencies? Are they small, mid-size, large, or global firms?

CATEGORY 2
What is the profile of your targeted customers?

a. Age

b. Gender

c. Profession

d. Income

e. Geographic location

f. Other demographics

CATEGORY 3
What are the major applications of your product or service?

a. For each major application, what are the requirements by customers?

b. What are the current ways of filling these requirements?

c. What are the buying habits of the customers?

d. What are the requirements of regulatory agencies?

e. Are your products/services bought by others to service their customers?

f. How does their industry look? How is their business doing financially?

CATEGORY 4
What is the impact (economic or otherwise) on customers who use your product or service?

a. How much will they save? What is their return on investment (benefit)?

b. Will they have to change their way of doing things?

c. Will they have to purchase other goods and services to utilize yours?

d. Will they change their work habits?

e. Overall, how will you satisfy their needs or wants better?

CATEGORY 5
What share of the market do you hope to capture?

a. What is the growth (historical and potential) of your market?

b. What are the market trends?

c. Is the market seasonal?

d. What factors will affect the market (economic, government regulation, etc.)?

CATEGORY 6
What are your market share objectives?

a. What are your market share objectives for the total available market?

b. What are your market share objectives for the service available market?

c. What are your market share objectives for the replacement market?

d. What are your rationale and costs of achieving different levels of market penetration?

e. How will you satisfy current customer needs?

f. How will you attract new customers?

g. How will you offer something new, better, or unique?

h. How will the segments and applications of your market change over the next three to five years?

CATEGORY 7
How will you distribute your product?

a. Will it be distributed under your name or someone else's?

b. Choose between direct, dealer network, wholesale, retail, or manufacturer's representative.

c. If transportation is involved, what are the implications of exporting? Importing? Taxes? Tariffs? Duties? Barriers? Foreign exchange and other concerns?

CATEGORY 8
What is the feedback from your prospective customers?

a. Have they tested a realistic prototype? How has feedback been incorporated into changes in your product/service?

b. Have you used focus groups and/or surveys to gather information from prospective customers?

c. Have you established a support/feedback system for your customers?

d. Are your service and warranty policies adequate and in keeping with regulatory requirements?

CATEGORY 9
What are your costs?

a. What does each product/service cost you to sell?

b. What does each product/service cost you to produce?

c. What have (will) your profits been (be) by product/service?

d. What are your sales figures?

e. What are your current sales goals by product/service? Number of units?

f. What is your sales volume in dollars?

g. Are your sales expectations in line with the manufacturing ability to produce your product/service?

h. Are your pricing, service, and warranty policies competitive in the marketplace?

The following is a suggested writing sequence for the Market Analysis section of your feasibility study.

Subheadings to include:

1. Target Market and Characteristics

2. Analyst Summaries

3. Market Share, Trends, and Growth Potential

4. Sales, Distribution, and Profits by Product/Service

TARGET MARKET AND CHARACTERISTICS

Using profiles, discuss how your product/service meets the needs of your target market(s). To do this, you'll need to describe your target market(s) and explain who or what is included, especially the buying records and habits of your customers. Be certain to include pertinent facts concerning the size, age, location/area, profession, income, and other demographic information about the market. If you have conducted studies or surveys to learn about your markets, refer to them in this section and include the entire survey instrument as an appendix to your document.

ANALYST SUMMARIES

Quotations and statements should make clear what problems and needs exist in your market. It should become evident to the reader that your product/service can solve these problems and/or meet these needs better than existing methods. The objective is to pinpoint specific market opportunities that exist within the industry and how your product/service capitalizes on these opportunities. Provide a series of quotations and statements that summarize significant facts, figures, and trends about the market (and market potential) from various reputable sources. Be sure you properly credit the sources and provide the date of publication.

MARKET SHARE, TRENDS, AND GROWTH POTENTIAL

Discuss the growth potential of the entire market and your increased share. State the assumptions on which you base these growth patterns (e.g., technology development, changing customer needs, costs). Discuss your rationale and the costs and risks associated with achieving higher levels of penetration. State the percentage share of the market you have or hope to gain. Discuss the trends of the market— industry wide, regional, and local. State whether the market is seasonal, delineate the time frames, and discuss how you will adjust and compensate during the off-season. Discuss how the market may change over the next three to five years.

SALES, DISTRIBUTION, AND PROFITS

Discuss your projected sales record by product/service. State how much each product/service costs you to produce, distribute, and sell. Discuss how your product/service will be distributed and sold. Describe any unique features of your sales and distribution network.

Discuss the implications of transportation, tariffs, duties, foreign exchange, and other government regulations.

WHAT TO WATCH FOR

One of most common errors is making unrealistic market share projections (believing you can capture 100 percent of the market, or even 50 percent), as is a failure to demonstrate a clear understanding of the product or service to be sold and to which market it will be sold. For example, it is unreasonable to assume that your customer base is equally distributed throughout the markets you plan to serve. Nor can you take for granted that your primary target market represents the major portion of the demand for your product/service (the 80/20 rule—20 percent of the customers may represent 80 percent of the demand). This sometimes occurs when you address your market universally by defining it too broadly, rather than segmenting your market into various components and developing specific profiles.

Another major error found in market analysis concerns sales projections and profitability expectations. These errors occur for several reasons: (1) failing to include an accurate estimate of the profitability of each product/service, (2) basing sales projections on a higher degree of output than you have adequately demonstrated can actually be met, and (3) establishing pricing that is not in line with target market needs, desires, or ability to pay.

A final critical oversight is not looking ahead in your market(s) to accurately anticipate future growth in demand for your product and/or service. This error occurs if you fail to properly assess the total market potential or changes in the market caused by economic, social, or other trends or if you fail to support target market assumptions in light of advances in technology, government regulations, population shifts, and economic forces (oil prices, interest rates, etc.)

SECTION 5: FINANCIAL FORECASTS

Without a doubt, the most difficult section of a feasibility study to write with confidence is the one concerning financial information. That's because so much of the mathematical equation is unknown or hypothetical at this early stage, so projections seem arbitrary at best. Yet without a benchmark for income, expenses, and revenue, it is difficult to move beyond the feasibility stage with the necessary confidence to build your business. One solution is to begin with the basics of start-up costs. Let's figure out what it will cost you to make what you hope to sell and then determine whether your market(s) can bear that cost.

If you plan to open your own business, you might as well also plan to spend your own money—lots of it—especially at the start-up stage. It is not uncommon for some entrepreneurs to turn to risky options, such as obtaining cash advances from their credit cards or home equity loans, at this stage as a means of self-funding their dreams. Although small business loans from banks and personal loans from friends and family certainly are possible, you need to create the opportunity for their investment by building your business from the idea to the prototype stage. To do so, you'll need to consider and budget for five categories of start-up costs that will be required for months, maybe even years, before you open your doors for business and begin to see revenue. Be sure to include someone on your management team who has solid accounting skills, particularly if you lack this competency, because spreadsheet savvy is critical at this stage. The five categories of start-up costs are discussed next.

1. WHO YOU'LL EMPLOY

As the visionary of your business, you may be willing to forgo compensation until income is generated. However, those who work with and for you may not have the means or desire to do so. It is possible to trade future equity in the business for start-up participation at low or reduced costs, but be sure to put this agreement in writing so that all parties understand the terms of the arrangement.

Some services you'll need to either master on your own, hire for equity, or outsource. Such services and providers include legal and accounting advice and transactions and any consultants who bring needed expertise that you and your core management team lack at this point. For example, to open a restaurant, you clearly need to compensate your chef(s) and wait staff as well as any other line service providers.

2. WHAT YOU'LL NEED TO MAKE AND SELL YOUR PRODUCT OR SERVICE

If you produce a product, you'll need to know the price of all components of that product as well as discounts and conditions applied to bulk purchases of raw materials. If you can save money by buying raw materials in bulk, you'll need to counter those savings with any additional costs required to store those materials until they are used. You'll also have production costs, which should proportionally decrease as your production volume increases. Products you create and retain for future demand are inventory, which will also incur an expense to store and manage, even though they are considered an asset. Packaging and shipping costs also are substantial and need to be carefully factored into the start-up equation.

For a service-oriented business, development costs can be easier to calculate and manage. In many cases, these costs are more arbitrary than those associated with products because they largely depend on the costs associated with your time and the time of your employees.

3. WHERE YOU'LL LIVE

Unless you plan to run your new business out of your basement or garage (the humble starting place for many successful businesses), you'll need to consider expenses for renting or purchasing an office, retail/showroom/storage space, and space to develop your product. Along with this decision comes the need to insure the property for theft, fire, or other types of losses to your property investment. Then there's the need to outfit yourself with office equipment—everything from desks to computers (with software, of course) to phones, light fixtures, and fax machines—to name just a few. If you will be transporting goods as a part of your business, you'll also need to look into some sort of reliable transportation (automobile or van) for your business.

4. WHEN YOU'LL HIT MILESTONES

The inherit passion of entrepreneurs can tempt them to want to achieve all their business goals as quickly as possible. However, fast growth of a new business can be almost as dangerous as slow growth, because your business may not be equipped to meet the demands of all its customers on an accelerated timetable. Even established businesses such as Toys "R" Us struggle with growth challenges: During its first holiday season (1998) of offering online toy purchases, the retailer was unable to keep up with high demand from Web shoppers. Consequently, many toys were not delivered by the Christmas Day deadline promised to shoppers. The following year, Toys "R" Us contracted with Amazon to handle its online toy division, resulting in a much more successful holiday retail season.

Effective management of milestones—or deadlines for reaching agreed-upon action items for your business—also is critical for successful negotiations with investors. It is not uncommon for investors to time capital infusion into businesses based upon their ability to hit milestones on or before agreed deadlines. This means that even if your contract calls for an overall investment of $500,000, you may see only percentages of that amount based upon your success in achieving stated action items. Missing just one deadline could void the overall investment contract, so it is essential to be cautious when assessing a timetable for growth. For example, rather than agreeing to sell a certain number of units by April 15, write the milestone with a completion date of the second fiscal quarter—thereby providing a few extra months of time to account for miscalculations or overly optimistic expectations.

Milestone management also includes a serious appraisal of inventory management. For service organizations this is a relatively easy task, assuming that you know—unequivocally—that the required labor is available when and where you need it. A product-based business needs to tread more carefully here. Key questions are what will the demand for your product(s) be once it hits the shelves? How quickly can you develop new product to replace what is sold? What components are required to create your product, and how quickly can you acquire them from your suppliers? How much inventory should you keep readily available, and how much can you develop using the just-in-time model? The answers to these questions certainly impact your start-up costs because funds invested in producing inventory are obviously not available for other necessities, such as marketing or administrative costs.

5. HOW YOU'LL MARKET YOUR BUSINESS

From business cards to shrink wrap, you'll need to consider how you present your business to the world. These costs add up quickly and are frequently the ones underestimated by new business owners. Besides business cards, you may need letterhead stationery, brochures, or other written material explaining the features and benefits for your product/service, as well as directions for appropriate use. Packing and shipping costs also can be overlooked—will you use boxes and mailing labels bearing your company name and logo? You will also need to spend money to promote your business through advertising, with costs that vary widely. A single newspaper ad might cost $250 to $300, whereas a television commercial could cost between ten and a hundred times that amount. A simple listing in the local telephone directory costs several hundred dollars per year. A company Web site will require initial investment of several thousand dollars to get up and running and then additional monthly maintenance fees. From billboards to radio spots and flyers to storefront signs, getting the name of your business into the marketplace requires a considerable upfront investment.

SECTION 6: MANAGEMENT TEAM

Your team is the heart and soul of your business—its members will implement the plan you are working so hard right now to develop. The old advice to "surround yourself with the smartest people you can find" definitely applies to start-ups. You are investing considerable time and energy to launch your business; expect nothing less of those who work with and for you. It is important to have business core competency skills close at hand in addition to those skills necessary to run any successful business (such as financial acumen and technical expertise). An honest assessment of skills in hand versus skills needed versus optimal skills desired is appropriate here, allowing you to develop a gap analysis of what your team has versus what it needs. One approach to bridging these gaps is to develop an advisory board for your business. This group consists of individuals selected for their expertise, experience, and insight in narrow but critical business spectrums. Physicians, college professors, engineers, scientists, or even fashion designers are potential advisory board candidates—let the nature of your business be your guide. Include biographical sketches of your advisory board in the Management Team section of the business plan. You also will want to include summarized professional biographies in this section as well as complete resumes as an appendix to this section.

NUMBER SEVEN—"I CAN'T DO THIS BY MYSELF"

Imagine trying to convince people to buy into the overnight squid delivery business. It's a lonely job, or at least it was for a while for Bryan Canepeel, CEO of XenoBiotics. His business provides high-quality marine bioproducts from Indonesia for use in pharmaceutical research. Unlike the other providers in this industry, he's figured out a way to get them from point A to point B—alive.

Suffice it to say he was in it alone in his venture from the start. "The business had more of a 'what good can I do for others besides make money' framework and origin," explains Bryan. "Collecting novel organisms from the sea for research purposes to aid in the discovery of new cures for human ailments seemed to be a rather worthy venture."

It also was "unique and puzzling" to investors, so Bryan had his work cut out for him. "The dynamics of importing time sensitive, highly perishable products in a highly regulated environment is difficult, to say the least," he explains. "Its amazing how ideas and communication can get transformed when not effectively managed."

On his own for 14 years, Bryan eventually knew that having a team around him could open more doors and opportunities. "I sought out the smartest people who were aggressive, not afraid of risk and were willing to work hard, "says Bryan. "The team members were also very committed to integrity and they were very unique, interesting people with amazing personalities."

So what would Bryan's advice be to entrepreneurs? "Our most interesting ideas are inspired from dreams or day dreams. Long rides in the car or going on a 3- to 4-hour walk gives us opportunities to reevaluate who we are and where we are going. Quiet time is the best source of good ideas.

"I recently heard one lecture on the importance and efficiency of spinning something new, or making a current operation more efficient with a workout program," he continues. "You don't always have to look for aliens. I suspect many of the answers facing society in the future are right in front of us in our current relationships and endeavors."

Bryan's experience in the trenches is a good source for anyone starting out on the path of building a new business. He suggests that all would-be entrepreneurs should: "Listen to your dreams, especially those that you remember as a child that reoccur in your later years. Don't be afraid to take a chance early as you can always recover later if it doesn't work. Having the guts today is what it takes. Be persistent! You're only a few failures away from cracking the code."

REVIEW

Five key points to remember are these:

1. A thorough feasibility study is a lot of work, but its completion enables you to move to the next stage of business plan development with confidence. Exactly like it takes money to make money, it takes time to figure out whether additional time invested in your new venture is well spent. Don't skimp on time in this tremendously valuable process.

2. A feasibility study is an internal document, an accumulation of information and data that will give you insights needed to take the next steps in developing your business. It will not be read by external audiences, so don't spend time polishing its prose. The writing process certainly helps in idea formulation, however, so don't skip this part entirely. The business plan is where you'll want to invest your efforts in a well-written and attractively presented document.

3. Do not feel frustrated if you seem to have more questions than answers within the major sections of your feasibility study, especially the financial section. That's quite normal at this point. You are actually learning what you'll need to know, which is much better than forging ahead without a map into unknown territory. The process of asking tough questions about your potential market and competition works as a trigger, enhancing your ability to uncover information in these areas.

4. Product businesses generally cost more to start than service businesses but also provide more barriers to entry against would-be competitors. However, "bootstrapping" is much easier for service than product businesses because the service is marketed based on the skills of the entrepreneur/ employees rather than the successful development of product prototypes. Either way, you'll need to pay close attention to your start-up costs to be sure you'll have enough financial resources to actually get the product or service to market.

5. If you don't have expertise in needed areas, develop an advisory board and "borrow" that expertise to help get your business off the ground. Surround yourself with intelligent and experienced people by compensating them with an equity stake in the business (as well as a salary if you can afford it). Even though you are the business visionary, you'll need a strong team around you to build your business.

ASSIGNMENTS

1. Using the approach outlined in this chapter, research and compile information as it pertains to each major section of your feasibility study. This information includes the following:

    a. Company and industry

    b. Product and service

    c. Competitive analysis

    d. Market analysis

    e. Financial analysis

2. Develop a list of names of individuals who you think would be assets on an advisory board for your business. Be sure to select individuals who have unique expertise and with whom you feel comfortable sharing proprietary company information.

3. Be sure your resume is up-to-date, as well as those of all members of your management team. Be sure to highlight skills from past employment that you plan to emphasize in your new business venture.

As you complete what will likely seem a mountain of work in this process, take heart that most of what you are working on is directly transferable into the business plan. That challenge awaits you and is presented in Chapter 3.

ENDNOTE

1. Feasibility material developed in collaboration with Professor Jeff Bernel, University of Notre Dame. Used with permission.

3 WRITE YOUR WAY INTO BUSINESS

The important thing is not being afraid to take a chance.
Remember, the greatest failure is to not try. Once you find
something you love to do, be the best at doing it.

—Debbi Fields, founder of Mrs. Fields Cookies

It's time to write your business plan. A business plan is not a novel, but it needs to be compelling and believable. Nor is it a term paper, but it needs to be precise, factual, and well documented. The business plan is a living document in that it will never really be completed. It is a work in progress that will evolve with your business and adapt to incorporate feedback from others who read it. But for now, it is a composite of the data mining you accomplished during the feasibility study phase. If you've thoroughly completed the assignments of Chapter 2, much of your business plan content should be in hand. The challenge now is to use that content to build a compelling story in support of your business idea and plan for implementation.

Most experts agree that your plan should not exceed 20 to 25 pages. It should be neatly prepared with logical section headings, single-spaced type no larger than 12-point type and no smaller than 10-point type, and in an easily readable font such as Times Roman. It will make liberal use of bulleted points and tables to display pertinent data. Of course, your plan will also include a cover page, table of contents, page numbers, and all necessary citations.

Following are the major section headings for a typical business plan. It is important to note that the order in which they appear is not the order in which you need to write them. We will spend the remainder of this chapter discussing each major section in detail. Feel free to jump into writing whatever section is most appealing to you or the section for which you have the greatest amount of information available. Business plan development is anything but a linear process. It also doesn't have to be a chore if you think of it in the right way—you are outlining the path for your future, and in doing so you can make it anything you want to be! You may think that you don't have time to write a business plan, but in fact you will waste time and money in the long run if you don't take this crucial step in developing your business.

NUMBER SIX—"I DON'T HAVE TIME"

There's an age-old expression that states: "Do what you love and the money will follow." It's also a great way to think about your time: Do what you love, and time will fly. Or turn what you love into a business, so you can spend your time making money and making yourself happy.

That's what happens when a gourmet cook opens a restaurant, or a fashionista puts up her shingle on an upscale boutique. And that's exactly what happened to Trent Rock and Colin Strutz.

Trent and Colin grew up around winter sports in Colorado and North Dakota. As they enjoyed their sports, they continually thought of ways that improvements to their snowboards could lead to better and more enjoyable rides. Axia Snowboards was formed when these young entrepreneurs were introduced to world championship professional snowboard riders Tommy Czeschin and Matt Lindemuth. Together, they visualized boards made with the best combinations of materials and processes, designs based on rider-generated feedback, and decked out with the hottest graphics. And then they made it happen.

Under the guidance and support of Tommy and Matt, Axia unveiled a complete lineup of men's and women's high-performance snowboards that employed unique materials like novel resin compounds, bamboo, hemp fiber, and carbon composites. In Axia's first year on the market, their professional and amateur riding teams won or placed in more events than any other factory team other than the current market leader, Burton Snowboards. In their second full year of production, with development complete, Tommy rode the second generation of his CZ Pro Model to the World Cup and U.S. National Championships.

Make time for your dreams, and make your business about the life you want to lead.

MAJOR BUSINESS PLAN COMPONENTS

Even though every business plan includes the list of elements presented below, there's absolutely no need to write them in that order. That said, there is a factor of natural sequencing at work here. Begin with whatever section for which you have collected the most information to date—most likely, that will be your description of company, industry, product, or service. It will be very difficult to write your marketing plan without having completed your market analysis, and you really can't do that without knowing who your competitors are. Your management team may be as simple as listing the names and credentials of people across the room from you, or as challenging as figuring out what types of people you need to seek out to compensate for gaps in your own education and/or experience. You will likely rewrite your financials at least twice, likely more, as you determine start-up costs, price points for products/services, break even analysis, etc. As obvious as this sounds, make sure your business can show a respectable profit within a reasonable amount of time—certainly no more than three years and preferably closer to one.

Here are the essential ingredients for any business plan. Each item is explained in detail over the eight following pages.

- Executive Summary
- Description of Company
- Description of Industry
- Description of Product or Service
- Competitive Analysis
- Market Analysis
- Marketing Plan (sales and promotion strategies)
- Management Team
- Financial Analysis
- Appendices

EXECUTIVE SUMMARY

Even though the executive summary appears first in the business plan, many entrepreneurs find it easier to write last, after they have completed their plans. That's because a good summary will concisely offer highlights of each section of your plan, with the exception of the appendices. Obviously, it is difficult to write highlights if you haven't worked out the details. You'll want to strike a balance here—offering enough description so that the reader can read only the executive summary and understand the key aspects of your business but not so much that it exceeds two pages of single-spaced text. See Appendix A for an example of an executive summary written for start-up company Flash Seats.

DESCRIPTION OF THE COMPANY

The description of the company is the section of the plan where you describe the decisions you have made about the formation of your company and other pertinent facts regarding its history and development. You'll need to include the company's name and address, legal status (sole proprietorship, limited liability corporation, or partnership), date of formation, and brief description of your business and industry type, along with a product/service overview. If you haven't made some of those decisions, it is acceptable to discuss your intentions using the future tense. Any significant milestones, such as developing a product prototype, testing your product with focus groups, or generating sales and profits, should be briefly mentioned here as well. If you have written a mission or vision statement, you also want to include them in this section.

DESCRIPTION OF INDUSTRY

No business can succeed in a vacuum, and your business will undoubtedly be affected by trends within your industry. Better to understand and plan for those realities at this stage than be caught off guard by them later. Through your feasibility analysis work you've gathered much of the information you will need for this section. Let's begin with answering five basic questions.

1. What life stage is your industry in? Is it a blank slate with lots of start-up companies, more mature but with room for growth, or a long-time, established presence with leaders in market share clearly defined?

2. How much competition is in your industry, how fast are the competitors growing, and what is fueling that growth? Based upon the industry's life stage and growth rates, how likely is it that more competition will enter the industry over the next 12 to 36 months?

3. Are you in more than one industry? For example, a spa that sells products and provides services competes both with hair salons, manicure/pedicure shops, and the local convenience store that sells shampoo.

4. Is this industry seasonal? If so, are there off-season opportunities to generate revenue? For example, Pimlico Race Track in Maryland is home to the Preakness, but also serves as the venue for large rock concerts on tour through the area.

5. What are the barriers to entering this industry? Although costs are a common barrier, other significant factors include government regulations or licensing requirements, product testing, or safety inspections, to name a few. Does your business meet these required criteria?

DESCRIPTION OF PRODUCT OR SERVICE

It is essential to include in your business plan a thorough description of how your product/service was developed, how it currently works, and in what capacities and at which milestones it will evolve. All components of the product or service need to be detailed here, as do the sources for those components. Lists of specific attributes of products and services work well here, with special emphasis on those features you consider to be proprietary. Inventory requirements and demands are also appropriate to include in this section. When possible, use visuals to show readers what a product looks like; this is especially important if you've developed or tested a prototype. You also will want to begin to explain how your product/service differs from that currently in the marketplace. There's no need for elaborate detail on this aspect, however, as that information typically presents itself in the marketing plan section of your document.

COMPETITIVE ANALYSIS

Probably the most important outcome of the competitive analysis section is to show the reader which other companies share the same market space as you propose to serve and how successful they have been in their efforts to date. As you do this, keep in mind that not all competition is created equal—differentiations in product/service quality, availability, and price play major roles here. Besides looking at existing competition, be sure to think about who else could enter your target market(s) and what it would take to do so.

In general, service-related businesses tend to have lower barriers to entry, making them easier to replicate than product-related businesses. Internet-based businesses also are easier to get up and running than brick-and-mortar ones. Be honest about your competition, and be thorough in evaluating its strengths and weaknesses in comparison with your own. But don't be discouraged—a market with no competition offers no opportunity. In the unlikely event that you find yourself in such a market, ask whether your business is premature, obsolete, or not something that customers want or need.

If you remember only one thing about competition, remember that you always have it, even if it isn't apparently obvious. The statement "We have no real competition" only serves to identify you as an amateur, so just don't say it. Don't even think it, because it is simply not true. Even if no other business is serving the geographic base of your defined market, the realities of e-commerce enable customers to shop online vendors with convenience and ease. And there's always competition for the disposable-income dollar—if your customers do not purchase your product/service, how else will they spend their money?

MARKET ANALYSIS

You should have collected demographic information for potential customers during the feasibility analysis stage. In addition to offering valuable insight into what makes your customers purchase one product or service over another, the market analysis also is essential information in the development of your marketing plan. One major error in this section is ambiguity. Defining market boundaries doesn't limit potential customers; it only makes developing a plan to reach them much more manageable. Too generic a market (for instance, all residents over the age of sixty who live in Tucson, Arizona) may falsely convey a market size that is larger than realistic. Besides basic demographic information of age, gender, income, marital status, occupation, level of education, ethnic heritage, family size, and home ownership status, you'll need to gather geographic specifics of an urban, rural, or suburban residency and the corresponding characteristics of those neighborhoods.

Another category of critical information is the understanding of how your target markets think about and spend money. What are their priorities? Priorities are largely tied to lifestyle choices, which in many (but not all) cases are tied to age. Teenagers may spend a large portion of their income at Best Buy, whereas their parents may be more likely found in Home Depot. Delving deeper, you can learn by gathering psychographic data how factors such as fear, self-esteem, and social status impact the purchasing decisions of your target market. In short, it is all but impossible to know too much about your potential customers.

MARKETING PLAN

The marketing plan section is where you take all the data you've gathered about your target market(s) and put them to work. You need to develop a sales strategy, including the best way to reach your customers, what to tell and show them about your product/service, how to get them to remember your product/service, and how to convince them to purchase your product/service on a continued basis. Low price points alone do not guarantee sales; if they did, subcompact car sales would regularly outpace SUV or luxury models, and Tiffany's would have gone out of business long ago.

Breaking down the sales process into three definable categories is a good starting point. These categories are presale, point-of-sale, and post-sale.

1. PRESALE: REACHING YOUR CUSTOMERS AND TEACHING THEM ABOUT YOUR PRODUCT

Product identification is a core component of a business identity and reputation. Through targeted advertising, you'll promote your logo and brand—shorthand versions of the company's mission, niche, and reason for existence—to potential customers. It is important to select advertising outlets where your customers already are congregated—few people go looking for marketing messages. Options include advertising in newspapers, magazines, or trade journals; on radio and/or television;

via Internet; or with brochures, posters, flyers, or billboards. Don't forget to list your business in the local telephone directory, and consider a blog if your product or service offers options for commentary. Besides the visual identification of your product, service, and business and their distinctive features, your marketing message should convey basic information such as price, features, and purchase location options. Your company Web site also should be easy to navigate, select items for the shopping cart, and check out with confidence and the knowledge that your customers' credit cards are protected by adequate firewalls.

2. POINT OF SALE: SELECTING YOUR PRODUCT/SERVICE OVER ALL OTHERS

Whoever said that "you can't judge a book by its cover" hadn't given much thought to consumer behavior. Very often, the "cover" or packaging of a product yields great influence on the decision to purchase one item rather than another. How your product/service is presented certainly will factor into the customer's decision to buy it, so be sure you give this marketing element considerable attention. For service items, provide a brochure or another written document explaining your policies, procedures, expectations for payments, and service guarantees.

All products should be tastefully and professionally packaged in a secure fashion to avoid tampering. The product cover should convey enough information for the consumer to make comparisons with alternate products, as well as price and other inventory data (retailers may take responsibility for some of these requirements). If supplemental products such as batteries are required to make your product work correctly, be sure that information is clearly displayed. Internal packaging such as brochures or fact sheets should include instructions for assembly and use, warranty/guarantee information, and company contact information should questions arise. Yes, you need to design and write all this material or hire a public relations firm to help you. Be sure to field-test all marketing materials to determine whether the results match those you were seeking.

You also need to give serious thought to the manner in which you would like your product or service to be sold. Thinking that you can do everything yourself is shortsighted; you're going to need some help. But with help comes training and compensation, which also require a bit of brainstorming. You also need to justify salaries for sales employees based upon reasonable expectations for your sales. Think about the role the salesperson plays in the decision process of your customers—will they need lots of help in understanding the product or service, or is it more or less self-explanatory? Does the product require a showroom environment to generate sales, or could it virtually sell itself on the Internet? Are telephone or mail-order sales an option, or will your products/services be sold through third-party retail outlets? You'll need answers to all these questions before making sales force hiring decisions.

3. POST-SALE: A REPEAT CUSTOMER IS (USUALLY) A HAPPY CUSTOMER

Unless your business holds a monopoly on a product/service, there is absolutely no guarantee of customers, never mind repeat customers. Yet they are the lifeblood of a business that survives the start-up stage to expand and move into stability. How can you ensure that your customers come back? Some important factors include the following:

1. Knowing who they are, via product or service registration or another means allowing for follow-up communication.

2. Ongoing communication via e-mail, direct mail, or other means announcing your business's new products and services.

3. Sending or providing samples of other related products and services to existing customers.

4. Inviting existing and potential customers to open house events at your business.

5. Developing and maintaining a company Web site so that new and existing customers can obtain additional product/service information with ease.

Probably the most important post-sale activity is one that you have little influence over but certainly could suggest to your customers. The tried-and-true "word of mouth" response to sales is most trusted and often used, making it essential that your customers have only good things to say to their friends about your business, products, and services.

MANAGEMENT TEAM

In all likelihood, you're reading this book because you have a great idea that you want to turn into a great business. That makes you the founder of your company. Congratulations—you've made it to the top. But just as a roof can't exist without a foundation, your business will be hard pressed to move forward without other key personnel. At a minimum, you'll need to surround yourself with people who possess core skills in each critical component of your business: marketing and sales, accounting, product and service research and development, human resources, legal, and technology, to name only a few major categories. Include a resume for each key personnel member in an appendix of your business plan, and be sure these resumes highlight skills for which each member is accountable in your business. Be sure to summarize key skills of each team member in the management section, however, because not all investors read appendices.

Knowing your strengths and weaknesses is essential here—are you a big-picture visionary with little patience for details? If so, you'd better have a staff to fill those gaps if you wish to be successful. If you've not already done so, consider taking the Myers-Briggs Personality Test to determine your professional strengths and weaknesses. Shore up your self-proclaimed weaknesses with the skills of others who report themselves strong in your weaker areas.

One way to augment your team's credentials is to add the skills and experience of an advisory board. This board comprises individuals who have high levels of experience and success in narrow but relevant areas to your business, products, and services. Their role is similar to that of consultants as you develop and launch your business. They also are a good source of contacts to funding leads as well as assistance on other essential matters. An advisory board differs from a board of directors in that the advisory board has no legal accountability to the company, and vice versa, and its members likely have invested time but not money in the start-up stage. Conversely, board of director members often have contributed financially to the company. During the early stages of the business, the board of directors may be made up of founding/key personnel. Once outside funds are accepted from angel investors or venture capitalists, the board demographics typically change to reflect these outside interests.

Another key objective of the management team section is to discuss how your business will be run day in and day out. This includes who reports to whom, key personnel responsibilities, supervisory functions and roles, and expectations for communication within the organization. One of the most complicated aspects of building structure in a start-up business is salary: How much will you pay yourself and those who work for you? Although it may be tempting to redirect all funds back into the business, the practical matter of how to support yourself is an ever-present conundrum. If you work elsewhere, you'll have alternate income but much less time to devote to your business. Your staff, although supportive, may not be in a financial position to forgo salary (even if they take an equity stake, stock, or stock options in the business, it still won't buy this week's groceries). Your example is important here—do not ask others to sacrifice for your business what you are not also willing to do without.

An additional element that can appear in the management team section of the business plan is milestones. However, because these deadlines for deliverables are commonly tied to financial objectives, you may opt to include them in that section instead. The logic for including them in the management team section is that milestones are directly tied to decisions made by key management personnel. What's certain is that without effective management, milestones are likely to go unmet. That's bad news if you're anticipating investment funding, as many venture capitalists make funding phases contractual and conditional upon reaching agreed-upon milestones within predetermined deadlines. Just one slipup from a team member could negate an entire contract and put future funding for your business in serious jeopardy.

FINANCIAL ANALYSIS

Although this section rarely appears first in business plans, it is often the section that potential investors first turn to when reading your document. In its simplest form, this section depicts where and how you spend money and how much you expect to earn as a result of doing so. Generally spanning three to five years in time, the data is broken down by month for the first year and quarterly thereafter. If you opt for a five-year forecast, it is generally acceptable to supply annual data for years four and five because the number of unknowns that impact start-ups tend to jeopardize the credibility of long-term financial projections.

The financial analysis section will include an income statement, balance sheets, cash flow statements, a summary of assumptions, a break-even analysis, and a description of the funding request and proposed use of funds. Start-up businesses lacking historical financial data will complete this section pro forma or by projecting expected financials into the future. Specifics of each section are described next.

1. *Income statements* simply show whether your company is making or losing money, which explains why this is also sometimes called a profit-and-loss statement. As part of this formula, income statements also show the distinction between gross profits (revenues less costs), labor and expense costs, and pre-/post-tax net income.

2. *Balance sheets* offer a record of a company's wealth in terms of its assets and liabilities. Assets are divided according to the type of items owned by the business (furniture, for example, is a fixed asset, as is land, computers, or buildings); owed to the business (accounts receivable); and cash, inventory, and any expenses you already have prepaid (current assets). Liabilities are what you owe as a business, including payroll and taxes, bills yet to be paid, and any long-term debt such as a lease payment. What's left over when you subtract liabilities from assets is net worth (let's hope this is a positive number) or equity, which gets added back into the balance sheet so that both sides match and add up to the same number.

3. *Cash flow statements* show how much cash is available to the business at any given time, yet they are calculated on a monthly and/or quarterly basis. That's not to say that cash isn't looked at very closely between reporting periods—some start-ups monitor their cash daily, if not weekly. To calculate cash flow, subtract all fixed expenses (such as rent and salaries) from available cash, and then subtract expenses that could be considered variable (advertising, office supplies). Be sure to take into account deadlines for your expenses. Your cash flow is the difference between what you have and what you spend each month. Sounds easy enough, but the challenge is figuring out how much cash will come from which sources, and when. One obvious but not always easy projection is cash sales. If you do not have a history of sales because your company is in the infancy stage, it's best to be extremely conservative here. Clearly, it's better to have more cash than you expected than less cash than you need. Also include cash that may come in the form of loans or loan repayments to you, as well as any credit-based funds available for use.

4. *Assumptions* are directly tied to the decisions that you are making in calculating your financial projections. They are the rationale for why you are projecting *growth* for your company and under what circumstances. How fast will your company grow? How quickly will you obtain target market share? How many people will you hire in what positions, and why? It's not enough to simply list dates and deadlines—you need to explain why you believe as you do and show any evidence that exists to help others draw similar conclusions. Throughout this process, remain true to your core competency as a business or you might make decisions that could harm rather than help growth in the long run.

5. *Break-even analyses* calculate, as the name suggests, the point at which the amount of money you've invested in your business is equal to the amount of money that you've earned. That's not to say that you are yet profitable, but you are no longer losing money trying to cover your monthly

fixed and variable expenses. To determine this figure, divide your monthly fixed expenses by your gross profit margin (which will take into account variable costs because they are subtracted from your gross cost of goods). Under some circumstances, you may wish to include this information in your "Assumptions" section, noted earlier.

6. *Funding request/use statements* explain how much money you have received from investors and lenders and what, in turn, you have promised to them (such as an equity stake in the company and/or stock options). Disclosure is important here—do not be tempted to "forget" to include loans from friends and family if they come with expectations for repayment or other conditions. If you have assigned a value to your company, it is appropriate to include that valuation in this section (but be prepared to have it disputed by investors!).

This section also outlines how you will use additional funds if they are obtained. Common uses are the expansion of staff and/or sales force, purchase of necessary equipment or inventory, expansion of the business into new geographic, product, or service areas, and increased marketing. (Note: Investors generally do not want to see their funds used to pay down preexisting debt.)

When you complete the financial analysis section, be sure to have an accountant or a likewise-trained financial professional review it for completeness and accuracy. You'll also want to regularly review this section—factors outside your control (such as shifts in the local economy) can impact pro forma statements.

APPENDICES

Appendices are not mandatory to your plan, but most entrepreneurs include them. Limiting the main business plan to 25 pages is a good idea because information overload can discourage some readers from reviewing your plan. However, you may have supplemental information you wish to share; if you do, this is the place to share it. Material commonly found in appendices includes diagrams and/or photos of products/services; letters of endorsement, resumes of key personnel, letters of intent from potential customers, results of customer surveys, a SWOT (*s*trengths, *w*eaknesses, *o*pportunities, and *t*hreats) analysis, details of manufacturing or technology contracts related to your business, organizational charts, or other contractual details too intrinsic for inclusion in the main document.

NUMBER FIVE—"I HAVE A FAMILY TO SUPPORT"

William K. "Billy" Boniface's family farm extends 400 acres tucked behind an old stone church in Darlington, Maryland. Home to 1983 Preakness Stakes winner "Deputed Testimony," Bonita Farm specializes in thoroughbred horse breeding, training and racing, and has been the Boniface family business for more than 30 years. The extended Boniface family lives in homes scattered throughout the Bonita Farm hilltops, which have the added benefit of being zoned in the Maryland agricultural preservation program. Kentucky Derby winner "Go For Gin" stands at stud while hundreds of mares and their weanlings idyllically graze throughout the valley.

The words "set for life" pop to mind. But due to radical changes in the horseracing industry in states surrounding Maryland, and the state legislature's unwillingness to take measures to remain competitive, the Boniface family has been forced to watch its industry and family business race to a crawl. As the industry has declined, Billy says that building a consensus within his family on how to deal with the situation has been tough.

"Change is difficult and can be scary," says Billy. "I try to be positive and see it as a new challenge. We're trying."

Despite the industry hardships this family business will survive due to the Bonifaces' willingness to think creatively and proactively about its most significant asset—land.

First came the Christmas trees, followed by two acres of grapes. If the horse business doesn't turn around soon, there could be organic beef cattle in Bonita Farm's future, or maybe even a winery. But there always will be a Bonita Farm. That's a factor of not only the family's diligence, but also careful planning.

"Business plan, business plan, business plan!" shouts Billy Boniface when asked about the most important element of any family business. "You need to set the goals and objectives of the operation and then review them on a regular basis to see if everyone is moving their divisions in the same direction. It's okay to take a detour but everyone needs to be on the bus."

Bonita Farm is set up as a partnership. The three brothers each own 20 percent of the operation while Dad and Mom own 40 percent. "This was done by design," explains Billy. "My brothers and I must all agree to move on any major business decisions without the votes of my parents but in reality, if Dad and Mom felt if the entire next generation could come to a agreement, they would support it."

"In the beginning, the three of us very seldom ever agreed on anything but as we have gotten older we have learned the importance of compromising to accomplish what we want," he continues. "The day-to-day operation and decision making of each of the three divisions of the farm is carried out by my brothers and me. Dad is still the general manager of the business with override authority, which he has exercised on very rare occasions. His style is more of jumping in where needed and providing guidance."

So what is it like sitting across from your coworkers at family meals? "When times are good and things are going well everything is great. When times are not so good working with family can be hard," explains Billy. "You place blame and say things to family that you won't normally do in a work environment. It is also hard to separate out business from family events. That makes Thanksgiving Dinner eventful at times."

REVIEW

This chapter breaks writing tasks associated with your business plan into distinct and manageable sections. These sections include the Executive Summary, Description of Company, Description of Industry, Description of Product/Service, Competitive Analysis, Market Analysis, Marketing Plan, Management Team, Financial Analysis, and Appendices. Do not be overwhelmed by writing an entire plan. Simply take one section at a time. Write in any order that feels comfortable to you, but rearrange sections to reflect the order described here prior to submitting your plan for review by investors and other audience groups. Keep in mind that business plans are "living documents" in that they are never really completed. Rather, they offer a road map for your business's development and growth. You'll want to revisit your business plan at least annually to see how your business achievements measure up to your projections.

ASSIGNMENTS

1. Begin setting short- and long-term goals for your business. Working backward, identify the goals you would like your business to achieve at month 36, 24, 12, and 6. Then make a list of what you need to accomplish to make each of these goals a reality. These are your action items.

2. Conduct a gap analysis of the skills possessed by your management team. Where is there overlap or deficiency? What are your team's strengths and weaknesses? Generate a list of potential advisory

board members based on desired skills and perceived weaknesses. This group can help fill those gaps until you have adequate funding to staff additional positions.

3. If you can gain access to other business plans, review them as potential models for your own. Although no two plans are the same, ideas for organizing content or useful appendix material are often transferable.

4. Taking each section in turn, write your business plan. When you have a draft that feels comfortable, share it with all members of your team as well as your advisory board, and ask for constructive feedback.

5. Challenge your plan by testing it for readability and completeness. One way to determine whether your plan is reader friendly is to read it aloud. If your plan's sentence structure mimics the natural pauses and breaks in speech, you're probably on the right track. If you're unable to read your sentences without gasping for breath, or if they sound stilted or awkward, you've likely written sentences that are too long, composed in the passive voice, or have too much extraneous information. Even with business plan writing, simple often works best.

4 ONCE YOU'VE GOT IT, FLAUNT IT

The only place where success comes before work is in the dictionary.

—Vidal Sassoon, entrepreneur

Audience analysis is critical to the development of any successful presentation plan. That is no difference in the presentation of a business plan than it would be in any other speaking opportunity. It is critical to understand audience group demographics and dynamics so that you can effectively anticipate people's questions, concerns, and likely reactions to your business idea. Learning retention research shows that audiences are 75 percent more likely to remember information if it is presented in a visual, aural, and written format simultaneously rather than in only one medium.[1] As a document author, you also face a challenge in determining what information to keep or eliminate as you move from a document that supports written communication toward spoken communication. This decision is based on who is in your audience, and what they need to know.

NUMBER FOUR—"I AM TOO YOUNG"

It was the spring of 2001, and two University of Notre Dame seniors had a problem. They were about to graduate, had no job prospects, and were out of beer. What they did have was resourcefulness, a dial-up Internet connection, and a few textbooks sitting around their South Bend, Indiana apartment. Having completed their exams, those books seemed to be just taking space. Xavier Helgesen looked at the books and then at his roommate, Christopher (Kreece) Fuchs. He had an idea. Xavier listed his books for sale on eBay, and to his surprise someone actually bought them. Kreece followed his lead, selling not only his used textbooks but all the ones he could gather up from other roommates and friends.

Had Xavier and Kreece believed that they were too young to start a business, this story would end here. But they didn't. A year later they decided to organize a book drive through which proceeds would benefit a local community center. Students donated more than 2,000 books, which generated $8,000 for the center.

Buoyed by their success, Xavier and Kreece sought the advice of another college roommate, Jeff Kurtzman, who had experience in investment banking and finance. Together they developed the business model for what today is Better World Books, a for-profit company with a social entrepreneurship mission to simultaneously improve worldwide literacy and decrease landfill waste. Five years later, Better World Books receives about 15,000 used books a day and sells about 5,000.

Now 28 years old, the founders of Better World Books have made a tremendous impact on the world. With 130 employees, this company—within the span of five years—also has accomplished the following:

- Collected over 10 million books from book drives at 1,200 colleges, universities, and libraries.
- Raised more $2.3 million for more than 80 literacy and education nonprofit organizations, of which $1.3 million was designated for Books for Africa. They also sent nearly 600,000 books directly to Books for Africa.
- Raised more than $1.2 million for libraries nationwide.
- Saved more than 5,250 tons of books from landfills.[2]

Incidentally, Michael Dell was 19 when he founded Dell Computers.

PowerPoint is a visual medium, but not all audience groups will see your presentation exactly the same way. It is very important that you figure out beforehand who will be in the audience while you're making your presentation, and adjust your slide content and sequencing accordingly. So what types of audience groups are you likely to encounter? Here's a typical, but not exhaustive, list.

1. Investors. You may recall from Chapter 3 the differences between them, but they all share a common bond in how your business will help them make money. Venture capitalists frequently consolidate resources in funds or firms and often are professionally managed and industry specific (investing only in technology-related or minority-owned firms, for example). They and angel investors (high net worth private individuals) will see your business in terms of its ability to grow quickly, be profitable, and build market share. Your friends and family may be more attuned to your dream of building your own business and are good sources for the start-up capital needed to get the business off the ground. With even the best written business plan, investors aren't interested in supporting good ideas. You'll need a prototype and some early success stories before securing a venture capitalist audience. Your financial projections also will need to be supported by solid assumptions and be based upon much more than "guesstimates."

2. Bankers. Although they likely look at the same success indicators as the above-mentioned group, they obviously are not investing their own money. They are bound by the standards of their lending institution, however. Having a respectable credit rating can't hurt with this bunch.

3. Partners. These individuals are looking for an appropriate match between their own personal interests and what you and your business offer. A potential management team member may possess a core competency skill that you lack yet need (accounting, for example) and share your dream of business ownership. Would-be advisory board members are professionals with narrow yet deep expertise in areas relevant to some aspect of your business. University professors often are called upon to fulfill this role.

4. Employees. As the proprietor of a start-up organization, you may not have the option of hiring people to work for you. Or, given the nature of your business, you may have no choice but to do so. Employees represent a distinct audience group that can make or break the success of your business. Although start-ups are not known for their ability to offer job security, that's precisely what many would-be employees will look for. Alternatively, they may wish to work their way into an ownership position within the business, a concept known as "sweat equity." They'll also look for opportunity for growth, with an assumption that as the business grows and prospers, their role will as well. An undeniable reality of start-up employees is that they are often asked to perform numerous duties and work well outside formal job descriptions. They'll also need to be comfortable with ambiguity, short deadlines, and shifting priorities.

5. Suppliers. It's important to analyze the level of interdependency between your potential suppliers and your business. To what degree is their success contingent on your own, and vice versa? Through that lens this audience group will assess your business's potential, strengths and weaknesses, and likely impact on their own business.

6. Customers. The familiarity of the sales process might make it tempting to view customers as the least daunting audience group. Customer perceptions of your business, however, are arguably your top priority. Perhaps your business idea evolved because as a customer, you could not find what you wanted or needed, or maybe you felt your skills could take an existing product or service and make it better. Feedback from customers at every stage of your business's life cycle is absolutely critical for your success. Be it early stage focus groups or feedback from repeat customers, careful attention to this audience group should always be an entrepreneur's top priority.

SHOW, DON'T TELL

After spending weeks or months digging down to the gritty details of your business, preparing for your presentation requires that you do exactly the opposite. To tell the compelling story that is unique to your business, you'll need to rise back up to the 35,000-foot level and look at your business from the different perspective of your distinct audience groups. You know more than anyone about your business, which is both a blessing and a curse. It may be tempting to assume knowledge on the part of your audience or take shortcuts in explaining assumptions for why markets exist. After all, you've spent months documenting these "truths"—isn't it only logical that your audience will agree with your assessment? Unfortunately, this is a dangerous assumption that entraps many entrepreneurs. The tendency to jump past rationales for why a business should exist is the first of several temptations you'll need to resist.

Fortunately, presentation software such as Microsoft PowerPoint is a helpful tool in organizing key points for business plan presentations. Its outline default mode encourages you to structure talking points from the broad to the specific, enabling you to create a story for the audience to follow. A balance between visuals and text complemented by your selection of talking points is the best approach. PowerPoint is a visual medium, capable of supporting a variety of content treatments. The trick is to select the most supportive approach to represent each section of your business plan.

An important note to mention is the recent trend by investors of asking to review PowerPoint presentations instead of, or in addition to, full business plans. It's worth considering putting together a second set of presentation slides solely for this purpose. What investors are really asking to see is your idea in a nutshell, evidence of a market, and a demonstration of how you plan to make money in that market. As simple as such a request sounds, that information can sometimes get lost in a 30-page business plan. The default of a bulleted PowerPoint list forces entrepreneurs to make hierarchial decisions about the importance of business variables, effectively deleting nonessential material. The problem is that these presentations tend to be text heavy, meant to be read rather than spoken. The best presentations allow entrepreneurs to combine their verbal explanation with visual representation, so these investor drafts are probably not what you would want to use in front of live audiences. However, if these additional PowerPoint slides serve the purpose of getting a potential investor excited about your idea, then they are worth the time of putting together as a business plan supplement.

As you prepare to discuss your business in front of various audience groups, you'll want to begin the slide development process by visualizing every aspect of your business—from the steps involved in completing a service, to product specifics, to cash flow, and audience demographics. Putting this in outline form is often helpful. You'll find that some factors will easily translate into visual components, such as those typically represented on a balance sheet or income statement. Others will be more complex, such as assumptions underlying a business premise that you have incorporated as justification for market share projections.

Don't assume that the way you've previously observed elements presented in presentations is the best or only way to display them here—you have lots of options to work with. Allow your content objectives (what you hope to accomplish by sharing this information with your audience) to determine the appropriate visual display rather than the other way around. After you've made your content choices and decided what visuals you'll need, then you can begin to imagine what they might look like. You have many graphic design elements to work with, including scanned images, maps, logos and icons, pie charts and bar graphs, Web site screen shots, video, and animation. Below are sample content objectives taken from a variety of start-up organizations to help you get started.

1. CONTENT OBJECTIVE: INTRODUCE YOUR COMPANY
The difficulty of this task is directly related to the type of business you are in. For a company such as Pepy Tours, a company that combines adventure travel and volunteerism in Cambodia, at least a hint of the nature of the business is inherent in the name. If Pepy was a traditional travel agency, the company would not need six slides to introduce itself. But Pepy is anything but conventional, and its founders

knew that investors would need to appreciate that difference before they would agree to support Pepy. As seen below, Pepy introduces itself by stating its mission and explaining how the Pepy experience works using testimonials of happy customers. It also shows how the Pepy model works, and why the demand for an experience offered by Pepy is significant and will continue to grow through the decade. Throughout the series of six slides, Pepy brands itself as a positive, upbeat, and happy company through its choice of bright colors, lively fonts, and smiling faces of Cambodian children.

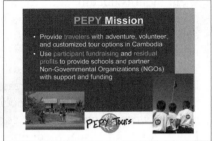

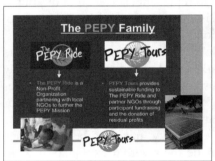

2. CONTENT OBJECTIVE: JUSTIFICATION OF MARKET DEMAND

You'll need to demonstrate a strong demand for the product/service you plan to provide. One option for achieving this is to document ongoing trends that support your market justifications. In this scenario, you are solving a problem either unmet or underserved by current product and service suppliers. Alternatively, you can show that your approach to meeting this demand is somehow superior to current market options, perhaps by being less expensive or more efficient. This objective is a logical complement to the business introduction and very often follows that section in sequence.

Globefunder needed to do this to become successful in the international micro-lending business it launched just three years ago. Its founders knew that their success hinged on their ability to synthesize an unfamiliar industry down to basics, and as such used a simple, uncluttered series of nine slides to justify market demand one step at a time. As they raised more than 2 million dollars prior to the launch, the approach obviously worked. As you can see below, Globefunder justifies market demand for its services by: (1) focusing on the magnitude of the market, with impressive loan payback rates of 95 percent, (2) showing the lack of competition in the form of a scalable distribution model with the exception of its own, and (3) clearly documenting how money is made at every step of the way.

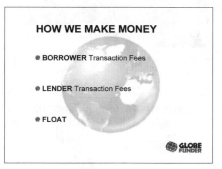

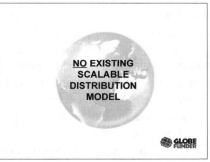

3. CONTENT OBJECTIVE: WHAT PROBLEM DO YOU SOLVE?

If your business justification is that the business solves a problem, it's logical to explain exactly how you plan to do this. You may also need to demonstrate that a legitimate problem really exists. Not that solving nuisances can't make for good business but clearly, the former situation creates a more immediate need within your marketplace. For a business such as Globefunder, the program was that borrowers and lenders could not access each other through traditional banking means, and individuals who wanted to invest in micro-businesses had few secure options in how to do so. Similarly, Pepy Tours offers an international travel and volunteerism experience to customers who likely would have struggled to created this experience on their own. Globefunder uses a sequence of five slides to show how it inserts itself into the micro-lending industry to bridge the gap of borrowers and lenders, whereas Pepy explains the not-for-profit version of that relationship in just a single slide. Be it five slides or one, they must be excruciatingly clear—if members of your audience can't understand how your business works, they won't be able to appreciate how you generate revenue.

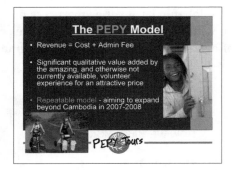

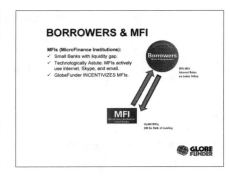

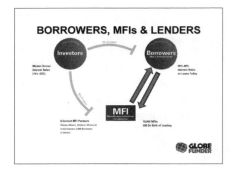

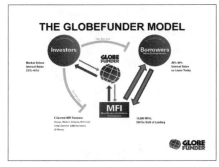

4. CONTENT OBJECTIVE: EXACTLY HOW DOES YOUR PRODUCT OR SERVICE WORK?

Do you have a patent? Have you invented a process? Now is the time to really show your audience how the core competency of your business works. You may use animation to demonstrate steps in a process or a series of slides accompanied by talking points delivered by you or another member of your business team. This is the approach that Por Fin Nuestra Casa used when it needed to explain its vision for how shipping freight containers could be refurbished and converted to secure, affordable housing units for poverty-stricken families living in the shanty towns of Juarez, Mexico.

A simpler approach is shown by Axia Snowboards, whose business model is based on a higher material quality/higher performance model for their products. Axia's "you get what you pay for" approach is tried and true, but this young company still needed to show why an investment in enhanced product, materials and process technology would result in better experiences for their clients. So they brought in Tommy Czeschin, the big gun in their industry, who happens to use an Axia snowboard. As a spokesperson, Tommy is the perfect fit for Axia, as his Olympic, world, and U.S. snowboard champion status certainly confirm the company's mantra that quality products equal quality performance.

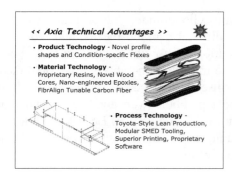

5. CONTENT OBJECTIVE: INTRODUCING YOUR MANAGEMENT TEAM

For Axia, there could be no better company spokesperson than Tommy Czeschin to gain instant credibility in the marketplace. But Axia was able to take this relationship even further when Tommy agreed to join the company's management team in a senior leadership role. And certainly images of Tommy using his snowboard to win competitions at the highest competitive levels has helped buoyed the company above its competitors in high-end sales. Investors know that as attractive and lucrative as any product or service might be, it's faith in the management team in which investments truly are made. Be sure to show off the skills and credentials of your team during your presentation with at least one slide that summarizes their skills and experiences. Have them in the room with you on presentation day if at all possible so that potential investors might meet them in person and ask questions specific to their expertise. If your team is young or lacks experience in vital areas, seriously consider forming an advisory board to help guide your business's growth and development. Certainly you'll want to share the names and credentials of these individuals with investors as well.

6. CONTENT OBJECTIVE: FINANCIAL FORECASTS

Probably the most difficult section of the presentation will be that devoted to financial information: start-up costs, sales and sales projections, and pro forma information (anticipated expenses, revenue, and income). A basic guideline is to move from the general to the specific as you explain your calculations and estimates. It's far easier for most audience groups to follow the reasoning (also called assumptions) that justifies your projections if you work from the macro- to the micro-level. This approach also will help you avoid putting too much information on a single slide—a tendency that also can overwhelm an audience. A progression of slides is your best choice, with each slide offering a deeper level of detail than the previous one. Also, just because this is the financial section of your presentation doesn't mean that it has to look like a balance sheet or income statement that you'd read in an annual report. There's only so much information your audience can absorb visually while using their auditory senses to listen to you speak—so resist the urge to overdo it here. Answer the basic questions and drill down to the details in the Q&A portion of your presentation.

If the purpose of your presentation is to request funding, it's a good idea to devote a slide to how much you are seeking and how the funds will be used. A simple text slide can get this job done clearly and effectively. As shown below by start-up company Xenobiotic, questions that must be answered in any presentation of this nature include: who will buy your product and why, what are they willing to pay and how do you know this, what do you need to pay to provide this service/product, what is the impact of cash flow concerns, and how will you make money in the short term and long term. In a nutshell, these are your revenue model and revenue drivers, and they need to make sense for everything else to fall into place. As seen below, this series of five slides answers these questions for Xenobiotic.

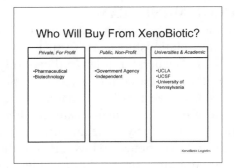

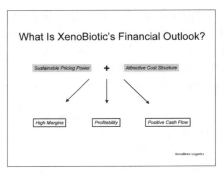

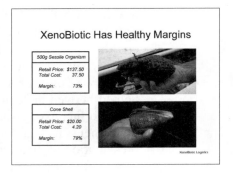

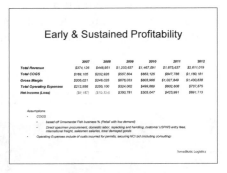

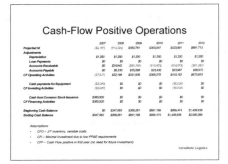

7. CONTENT OBJECTIVE: COMPETITION AND YOUR MARKETPLACE

A common error for new entrepreneurs is underestimating the breadth and depth of competition. Perhaps there's no other business exactly like your own, but you certainly are competing for the disposable income of your customers. You need to find out absolutely everything you can about the customers you hope to serve, and the businesses that are/were taking care of those needs prior to your entry to the marketplace. What did those customers buy before you entered the market? How much did they pay? Which companies served their needs? What are the alternatives to your product or service? These are only a few of the questions you should have answered in your feasibility study. During your formal presentation, you'll likely only mention the names of companies you consider to be competitive and offer brief reasons you believe that to be the case. A Q&A session may trigger more specific inquiries from audience members, however, so be ready to go into detail about competitors' strengths and weaknesses. Overall, you are on stronger ground if you focus on the strength of your company versus the weaknesses of competitor products/services. As seen below, Axia focuses its presentation on its ability to tap into a broad cross section of a high-end niche market, whereas on-line ticket exchange provider Flash Seats chooses to highlight its competitive advantages in a highly fragmented market.

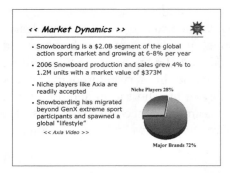

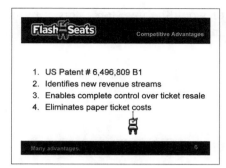

8. CONTENT OBJECTIVE: MILESTONES

You will need to demonstrate how you will implement your business plan, including a timeline for when you expect to reach certain goals. These milestones can be displayed in a number of ways. The only two essential elements are dates and goals. A good approach involves showing where and how goals overlap and what required steps are assumed along the way.

Your milestones also may be extended to show how customers may evolve as they use your product and/or service. They also should include an exit strategy where applicable. As shown below with the Flash Seats presentation, a single slide or two can cover this territory quite nicely. For the complete Flash Seats business plan and corresponding presentation please see Appendices A and B.

9. CONTENT OBJECTIVE: THE Q&A SESSION

An effective way to prepare for any persuasive speaking opportunity is to anticipate the types of questions your audience is likely to ask. If you are a nervous presenter, you may find it comforting to develop slides with material that supports logical questions for your audience to ask. This exercise also helps you check your presentation (and business plan) for completeness. Supplemental slides also give you the option of customizing your presentation on a moment's notice by simply changing the slide order using PowerPoint's slide sorter feature. The challenge is to keep track of all your slides so that you can find the appropriate data for responding to specific questions. A good directory with extensive use of hyperlinks within related slide material can help you organize your material by major category and then clustering related slides within each category. This approach allows you to move quickly and seamlessly though large volumes of support material.

ORGANIZING YOUR PRESENTATION

Your slide sequence is directly related to the specific group in your audience and how much time you have to spend with them. Chapter 5 will further define strategies for talking with various audience groups and incorporating their feedback into your business. For now, let's focus on a typical sequence of slides for a presentation to an audience of would-be investors. This is by no means a mandatory order—just a dozen slides that work well in many speaking situations.

1. Cover slide

2. Problem/solution description

3. Executive summary or mission statement

4. Description of product/service

5. Description of market

6. Overview of competition

7. Go-to-market strategy

8. Timeline for milestones

9. Financial forecast

10. Management team credentials

11. Exit strategy

12. Conclusion and call for questions

FINISHING TOUCHES

Much as you'd edit a text document prior to submission, you also need to carefully review your Power-Point slides for a number of critical factors.

1. Readability. Is the type and font legible? Can your audience clearly see the numbers contained in tables and charts? Can those sitting in the back row read the text without squinting? (If you don't have an answer for this, try to make it readable from about 20 feet.) Type that is too large also can be distracting, as can too much of any size of type on a single slide.

2. Visual impact. The goal is not to underwhelm your audience. Does your presentation convey the energy and excitement that investors look for in entrepreneurs? If your presentation needs jazzing up, trying adding text or image builds, color, or perhaps a bit of animation or video to the story. Avoid the long lists of dates, long lists of bullets, and long lists in general.

3. Overkill. Does your presentation go too far? For example, just because you can include audio in your presentations doesn't mean you want to. Sure, if you're in the music business, audio makes sense—but sound clips that herald the arrival of every slide can become annoying quickly.

4. Completeness. You'd use a focus group to generate feedback on your product or service, so why not also do so with your presentation? You want to be sure that you're not leaving out material that the audience really wants to see and that the material you've included is what the audience really cares about. Use friends, family, roommates—anyone willing to sit still for about 20 minutes and remain objective can work here.

5. Clutter. The most likely candidates for information overload are the financial section and graphics that try to squeeze too much information onto a single slide. Overall comprehension will be better if you take several slides and build on key points rather than jamming lots of data, text, and visuals onto a single slide. That approach makes the audience members work too hard because they are forced to repeatedly scan their eyes back and forth over the material to determine meaning. Sometimes less really is more. To paraphrase an old expression, "When in doubt, leave it out" (but put it in the Q&A slide section just in case).

NUMBER THREE—"I AM TOO OLD"

By his own account, Jeff Bernel, age 63, has been trying to retire for at least a decade, and he still hasn't figured out how to make it stick. But that's perfectly fine for this born-again chairman of Unitek Sealing Solutions of LaPorte, Indiana, because he's made his peace with the greener pasture on the other side of the fence. Or in Jeff's case, the bluer ocean.

By Jeff's own account, he's retired three times—once from the United States Navy, again from his position as CEO, President, and Chairman of the Board of American Rubber Products, and a third time as a professor of business at the University of Notre Dame. Six months of reflection time on his sailboat came next, with a subsequent realization that "there's got to be something more," he explains. "There are people who take and there are people who give, and I just like being someone who gives."

In July 2006, Jeff purchased a subcomponent of American Rubber Products, named it Unitek, and in doing so, saved it from certain foreclosure and its employees from losing their jobs. The company manufactures products such as rubber seals for automobile doors and trunks, windshield wipers, and other tubing and gasket products. "I wanted to help these people and I believed in what this company could do," says Jeff. "I wanted to become that invisible hand in the marketplace that could make a real difference."

He also found himself lured back to the Notre Dame classroom, where his love of teaching and the overall education process keeps him engaged everyday. "People really underestimate the value of a great education," he says, explaining that the network of peers you build through that process will create life-changing opportunities for many years beyond your time in class.

Jeff cites two characteristics as essential to all entrepreneurs: passion and persistence. "Most people give up when things get really hard because they don't have an internal control that allows them to figure out how to work around the walls," Jeff says. "I really believe in Unitek—my intuition told me this was a good thing to do. But before I had that gut check moment, I ran the data and researched absolutely everything. And then I researched it again. And then again."

Jeff teaches his students the practice by which he lives, which begins with never falling in love with just an idea. "Of course it all begins with an idea and ideas are essential," he explains. "But you can't work your idea in a vacuum—you have to pay attention to what the marketplace is telling you. Don't be afraid to make changes to that idea based on what you learn along the way."

Good advice from someone who has made a practice of redefining the idea of retirement. It's also exactly what Ray Kroc did in 1954, when he launched the first McDonald's restaurant in Des Plaines, Illinois. He was 56 years old.

REVIEW

You should now have some ideas for how to design professional slides that have visual impact. Always begin with your audience in mind, and be cognizant of any time restrictions on your speaking window. Let your content drive the selection of visual media rather than the other way around. Be sure to try out your presentation. Get feedback on whether it really shows the story of your business and answers potential questions of your audience.

ASSIGNMENTS

1. Create a storyboard for your presentation. This is a visual outline of how you envision your presentation to look. Try out different visual packages (pie charts, maps, bar charts, etc.) to see which medium conveys your data in the most interesting and compelling manner.

2. Create a "master slide" to use as a backdrop for all your related presentation material. This slide should incorporate any logos or product images you wish others to associate with your business. Experiment with colors and fonts until you find a combination that best represents how you wish others to perceive your business.

3. Even if you haven't finished your business plan, go ahead and begin to draft your presentation slides. You needn't work on these slides in any given sequence because their order is easily changed. Simply be sure that every major section of your business plan section has at least one corresponding slide in your presentation (for some sections, you'll likely have two to three slides or even more).

4. Try practicing your presentation with different time variations. Develop separate 10-, 20-, and 30-minute versions. Practice in front of an audience to gather feedback and gain experience in answering questions.

ENDNOTES

1. J. S. O'Rourke, *Management Communication: A Case-Analysis Approach,* 2nd ed. (Upper Saddle River, NJ: Prentice Hall, 2004), 99–100.
2. "Our Impact." Retrieved from http://www.betterworldbooks.com/Impact/Default.aspx.

5 TAKE YOUR PLAN ON THE ROAD

I have far more respect for the person with a single idea who gets there than for the person with a thousand ideas who does nothing.

— Thomas Edison

This is one of the most exhilarating aspects of starting a business: sharing your dream with others. Not only will your plan fall under tremendous scrutiny during this phase, but so will your ability to lead and manage your business. A good idea is only that, unless the person designated to execute it has the skills, savvy, patience, and persistence to finish what was started in developing the feasibility study and writing the business plan. That person is you, but you'll need to convince other key audience groups of that fact if you hope to obtain their support as you proceed from here.

Chapter 5 will help you accomplish these goals. In this chapter, we will review common venues for business plan presentations, from elevator pitches, to competitions, to potential investor meetings. We'll also further discuss the presentation process, with a special emphasis on how to appeal to the needs of the audience groups you are most likely to encounter.

NUMBER TWO—"I CAN'T BUILD A BETTER MOUSETRAP"

What do professional basketball and a book on business plan writing have in common? Josh Francis, and the plan he helped write for a company called Flash Seats. Josh needs to go only as far as the Cleveland Caveliers Web site to see how the start-up team and company he helped launch two years ago is up and running.

"The thing that stands out to me is not just finding unsolved problems or better solutions, but finding someone who is looking for answers and waiting to pay for solutions," explains Josh. "Great ideas are wonderful, but you need to keep asking who will pay for this? And keep in mind that the person who pays is not always the end user—that was the case with Flash Seats."

Flash Seats' technology and processes replace physical tickets for large sports and entertainment events with electronic ones, and offer a secure, online marketplace for transferring and selling tickets in a digital format. It also is an online market exchange tool for individual ticket holders to sell unwanted tickets to events to would-be buyers. Think scalping meets eBay and you'll have the general idea. The Cavaliers are the first team in professional sports to use this new technology.

Although these transactions could take place without technology, the online market certainly broadens the pool of potential buyers and sellers. And in the post–9/11 homeland security market, knowing the identity of who is sitting in what seat also is of great appeal to sports franchises, says Josh.

"We had to face and answer the question: 'Why would vendors care about this service? They have all of the tickets, so why would they need us?' said Josh. "The answer is that they do not profit on scalped tickets, nor do they know into whose hands those tickets may fall."

The Cleveland Cavaliers purchased Flash Seats in 2006, and it has been facilitating electronic ticket exchanges among fans ever since.

"A big part in inventing a better mousetrap is to look at best practices and proven ideas across different industries, and then put them together," continues Josh. "But once you have that better mousetrap, then you need to make your case for a value proposition."

ELEVATOR PITCHES: NOT JUST FOR ELEVATORS ANYMORE

Making your case—that's really the point behind elevator pitches. Although the idea of running into someone in an elevator sounds like the ultimate impromptu speaking opportunity, it is really necessary to give this chance meeting some serious thought in advance. Networking options exist everywhere, so having a concise but effective way to explain your new business is definitely in your best interest. You never know who you might meet while standing in a line at a coffee shop, whether they'd be interested in your plans, or whether they know others to whom they could refer you. There's even an annual competition for elevator pitches hosted by the Babcock Graduate School of Management at Wake Forest University. Be it completely spontaneous or a bit more formal, you certainly wouldn't want a great networking opportunity to slip through your fingers only because you couldn't figure out what to say. Memorizing a 30-second shorthand version of your business plan just makes good sense. Have longer variations of the pitch ready to go as well, from 60 seconds to as long as 4 minutes (just in case you find yourself riding the elevator in Chicago's Sears Tower).

So what are the ingredients of an effective elevator pitch? You won't close any deals during this conversation—all you can hope to accomplish is to generate an initial interest and try to obtain an opportunity for a longer follow-up discussion. Keep everything simple and conversational—this is no time to review the intricacies of your competitive analysis or test out your thesaurus. Answer the basic questions: What is the heart and core of your business, and why will it be successful? Remind yourself that enthusiasm and energy often are contagious and go a long way in obtaining subsequent appointments. Following are several additional elements you'll want to think about as you draft your elevator pitch.

1. What problem does your business solve? Alternatively, what opportunities does it create? Does it save time, money, or both?

2. Why should anyone care? How has your targeted market(s) gotten along until now? How does your product/service simplify or enhance your market's lives in some positive manner?

3. What is special or unique in your approach to this business? Do you have skills or experience that you can draw on to make improvements in the status quo? In a succinct fashion, you'll need to explain why you are credible and why the person you're speaking with should believe your pitch.

4. Is your pitch motivating? Why would the person you are speaking with want to set aside additional time with you to learn more?

5. Can you make money doing this? Show early successes in terms of sales, product demand, and customer feedback about potential improvements to product and services.

6. Can you prove everything you just said? How have you established your credibility with your customers in terms of product and service guarantees? Who can offer references on your behalf? Are there sources of third-party credibility (analysts or the media) that can verify your market size, business impact, and sales potential?

Finally, you also are responsible for establishing closure for the elevator conversation. This means that you'll inquire about setting up an appointment to speak further—in person or by telephone—at a later date. Be sure to print professional business cards and carry them everywhere. They provide a convenient means to share contact information. Offer your card, extend a handshake, and thank the person for the time they have spent with you, no matter how brief. If you've been invited to initiate follow-up opportunities, do so at your earliest convenience.

Here's a sample elevator pitch to get you started:

Hi Dr. Stanson. I just read the interview that the Maryland Gazette published about your new concept for "hometown residential" developments. I was absolutely fascinated with your vision to help reconnect families who have virtually distanced themselves. I agree that the time has come for all of us to step away from our laptops and Blackberries and reconnect with each other. My name is Daniel Smith, and I would love to talk with you about opening my bookstore café business in your new community. Unlike other cafes, ours purposively does not offer wireless service to our customers because we want them to interact with each other instead. We also plan to offer a seminar series based on what interests are exhibited by those who live in the surrounding community. May I give you my card and contact you next week so we can talk more about our common goals?

BUSINESS PLAN COMPETITIONS

If you are a student at the secondary, undergraduate, or graduate levels, or even an alumnus of business degree-granting institutions, you likely have access to business plan competitions. These are formal competitions that give you a chance to compete for cash awards, access to venture capitalists, high product and service visibility, and public relations, or all the above. You'll find numerous opportunities to become involved in these events, although many have criteria that you must meet beforehand. Arguably, the most prestigious competition is the by-invitation-only Moot Corp., sponsored each May by the McCombs School of Business at the University of Texas at Austin. Called "The Super Bowl of World Business Plan Competitions" by *Business Week*, this 23-year-old annual event is open only to first-prize recipients of other approved competitions affiliated with MBA programs around the world. Awards include $100,000 in cash prizes to top finishers, and participants have the opportunity to meet (and deal) with prominent venture capitalists, many of whom serve as judges.

Although the majority of competitions are associated with academic programs, the Small Business Administration[1] offers similar experiences throughout the country, as do some state and regional government offices. Presented in Table 5.1 are lists of prominent business competitions in the United States. The key features offered by major competitions appear in Table 5.2. A list of additional competitions is found in Appendix C.

MEETINGS WITH POTENTIAL INVESTORS

Finding the right investor at the right time under the right terms is tricky, at best. Early stage businesses often start with a "friends and family" round, which, as the name suggests, means acquiring funds from those closest to you. Assuming these funds are a loan and not a gift, it is extremely important to document the transaction for future reference. You don't want to become "persona non grata" at Thanksgiving dinner, so take these funds as seriously as any you would obtain from outside, third-party sources.

Depending on how deep these pockets are, you may be able to develop a significant portion of your business without needing additional outside funds. A general rule of thumb should be to not borrow money until you absolutely have to do so, and then negotiate the best terms as possible keeping in mind your demands for cash flow, inventory projection, staff hires, and so on. A small business loan from a local bank is often the next step in the funding process, as this transaction can be completed by paying interest rather than equity. If your business is deemed too risky or your cash needs too great, you may quickly move along to two additional options: angel investors and venture capitalists.

Table 5.1 Major U.S. MBA Business Plan Competitions	
Competition Host	**Competition Name and Date**
University of Georgia	**Georgia Bowl® Competition** First or second week of February
Indiana University	**Spirit of Enterprise Competition** Third week of February
University of California Santa Barbara	S.E.D. Business Plan Competition Early spring
University of Nebraska	**Info-USA Business Plan Competition** Fourth week of February
Carnegie Mellon University	**International Business Plan Competition** March
Boise State University	**Northwest Business Plan Competition** March
San Diego State University	**International Venture Challenge™** March
Wake Forest University	The Elevator Competition Fourth week of March
Rice University	**Southwest Business Plan Competition** March
University of San Francisco	**International Business Plan Competition** April
University of Oregon	**New Venture Championship** Second or third week of April
Purdue University	Life Sciences Competition Third week of April
Carrot Capital	*Carrot Capital Business Plan Challenge* April
MBA Jungle	*MBA Jungle Business Plan Competition* April
University of Texas	International Challenge of Moot Corp® First or second week of May

Key: Competitions listed in regular type are hosted by academic institutions.
        Competitions listed in italic type are hosted by nonacademic organizations.
        Competitions listed in bold type send their winners to Moot Corp®.

Source: "AACSB International." Retrieved July 10, 2004, from http://www.aacsb.edu/conferences/.

Table 5.2   Key Features of U.S. MBA Business Plan Competitions

Competition	Competition Focus and Uniqueness
Georgia Bowl® Competition (first or second week of February)	Its unique scoring system focuses on actual start-up feasibility. Top two semifinalists in each bracket go to finals.
Indiana Spirit of Enterprise Competition (third week of February)	A one-day competition that emphasizes reality in the plan's details. If your numbers are wrong, you're gone.
S.E.E.D. Business Plan Competition (third week of February)	A new competition that deemphasizes the team's written plan. Focuses on feasibility and venture upside potential.
Nebraska Info-USA Competition (fourth week of February)	Third oldest national competition. Focuses on start-up feasibility. Holds an undergraduate competition at the same time.
Carnegie International Competition (first week of March)	A new competition. Focus is not yet clear.
Boise State Northwest Competition (third week of March)	Second newest competition. Open to eight northwestern schools plus "at large" entries. Holds undergraduate competition at the same time.
SDSU International Venture Challenge™ (third week of March)	Second oldest national competition. Has wild-card opportunity for all second-place teams to advance to finals. Has five open slots.
Wake Forest Elevator Competition (fourth week of March)	Make two pitches in two two-minute elevator rides to advance to finals and do a full pitch to four North Carolina venture capitalists. Nonstudents okay in finals.
Rice Southwest Competition (fourth week of March)	Strong venture capital emphasis. Fifteen-plus judges in all first-round brackets. Best #2 gets wild card to finals. Forty-five plus final-round judges, mostly venture capitalists.

continued

Competition	Competition Focus and Uniqueness
USF International Competition (first week of April)	Plans deemphasized. Elevator pitch to venture capitalists to determine semifinal brackets. Finalists pitch to California venture capitalist panel.
Oregon New Venture Championship (second or third week of April)	Environmentally friendly plans favored. Has prize for best fast-pitch presentation. All slots except five are open to any school.
Purdue Life Sciences Competition (third week of April)	All entrants must qualify on written plans. Emphasis is on biotechnology, medical devices, and health services.
Carrot Capital Business Plan Challenge (fourth weekend of April)	Must submit business plans. The top twelve teams invited to New York City for presentations. Most top teams are offered term sheets.
MBA Jungle Business Plan Competition (fourth week of April)	Must submit executive summaries to MBA Jungle. Top teams are invited to California for the competition.
International Challenge of Moot Corp® (first or second week of May)	The biggest and oldest of them all. $100,000 convertible preferred loan to winner to help get venture started.

Key: Competitions listed in regular type are hosted by academic institutions.
Competitions listed in italic type are hosted by nonacademic organizations.
Competitions listed in bold type send their winners to Moot Corp®.

Source: "AACSB International." Retrieved from http://www.aacsb.edu/conferences/.

Angel investors are high-net-worth individuals who may be considering an investment of their private funds, or work as a member of a smaller consortium or a fund collective. Venture capitalists often consolidate resources in funds or firms and often are professionally managed and industry specific. As audience groups, they share characteristics of being direct, extremely busy, and impatient with fluff, spin, or conjecture. A meeting with either audience is certainly a big step in the right direction, but it's a long way from guaranteed funding. In fact, guarantees are few and far between—you may not even have five minutes to present your formal presentation before this group before being interrupted with questions. Increasingly, angels and VCs are forgoing a total review of your business plan in favor of a copy of your PowerPoint slides and an attached executive summary. Your survival and success before this group will depend on being specific yet succinct, and you will not be granted a second opportunity to meet with them if your first impression is anything less than stellar. It's simple supply and demand—there are far more would-be businesses than investors to fund them, so this group can afford to be picky.

QUESTIONS AND ANSWERS ON Q&A

Business plan competitions often incorporate Q&A components into the presentation requirement. It is essential that you prepare for this speaking opportunity as much as for the formal presentation, but in a different manner and with different goals. Your tone and choice of words can be as important as the information you choose to share. Avoid being overly submissive, defensive, or aggressive in front of the judges. And remember that sometimes judges' questions and concerns will be the most valuable lesson you'll learn in the contest.

GUIDELINES FOR SUCCESSFUL PRESENTATIONS

Regardless of speaking venue or purpose, you should keep in mind a number of common "do's and don'ts" as you proceed with your presentations. It's not enough to simply have a great idea committed to paper with the statistics to back it up—it's time to sell that idea and convince your audience that you and your team is the best choice to make this business a reality. Yes, you've done all the hard work, but no, you can't hide behind it. Here are eight "make or break" tips to make your presentation a success.

DO'S

1. Make it personal. Try to find out as much as you can about each individual you will be speaking to beforehand. At a minimum, know names and titles. If possible, introduce yourself personally to each audience member before you begin to speak. Gathering helpful anecdotes such as where they live or attended school also can give you options for personalizing presentation content to the group.

2. Be organized. Tell your audience in advance how you plan to proceed through your presentation by giving them a road map in the form of an agenda or overview slide. This need not take more than 90 seconds, but it helps them organize the sequence of events about to unfold. You may want to consider using a "frames" approach to your PowerPoint presentation, designating a margin of each slide as a miniature outline for key discussion points.

3. Be considerate of their time. Tell them how long you will speak, and then keep your word. In general, shorter is generally better, and by short we're talking 10 to 20 minutes. If more time is available, allow your audience to drive the discussion by offering lots of time for questions and answers. You should know that many investors will be unlikely to allow you to finish your formal presentation before beginning to ask questions. You'll need to adjust your format quickly to adapt to their expectations. Having smaller, interchangeable PowerPoint options enables you to change gears quickly without appearing disorganized or confused. Certainly, this approach allows your audience to see firsthand how you handle stress.

4. Open and close strongly. First impressions are vitally important in entrepreneurial speaking opportunities. Simplify your business idea so that your audience can get excited about it quickly, and then rally your audience around the key factors of market impact, demand, and profitability. It is your job to concisely explain elements to which you may have devoted dozens of pages in your business plan. It is also your job to connect the dots within your business plan—don't make your audience guess how one aspect relates to another.

5. Speak in clear, plain English—no technical gobbledygook, acronyms, or insider jargon. Use the strongest speakers on your management team to present your material in the main presentation—content experts (marketing, sales, accounting, etc.) always can be called upon later to answer more technical questions. Finally, be sure to close each segment of your presentation with a strong summary of key points. Don't force your audience to remember what you assume to be most relevant, and don't assume that the audience's definition of relevance is automatically the same as your own.

6. Capture your audience with content. As mentioned in Chapter 4, you want to show off your product or service whenever possible in a presentation. Got a prototype? Bring it. Have a Web site? Link to it. Can a DVD clip capture the spirit of your new venture? Show it. Demonstrate the impact of your product/service on your chosen market with written testimonials from actual customers (or focus group members). Offer credible evidence to support why your product/service is needed within the market(s) you plan to enter. In short, do whatever it takes to show that you have long surpassed the "idea" stage and have evolved into a real, visible business with bona fide products/ services actually engaged in the marketplace. Be sure to convincingly answer the critical questions that any investor would ask: "Who needs this and why?" and "Why you? Why now?"

7. Exude enthusiasm and confidence. No one in the room should be more excited than you are to discuss this material. Use lots of eye contact, and connect with everyone in the room at least once. Be sure your speaking voice is strong and clear. Watch that your pace of speech isn't too rapid (nerves can accelerate speaking rates) or monotone—you want your audience to neither struggle to keep up with you nor lose interest.

8. Be Q&A savvy. Yes, this point is listed multiple times because it so often makes or breaks meetings with investors. Each audience member has an agenda, which often reveals itself through the choice of questions asked. These questions are actually clues as to the concerns about your business that exist for your audience. Your answers either help allay these fears or compound audience concerns, so be sure it's the former. Ample preparation for presentations can help you anticipate many likely questions and subsequent answers, which can only work to have you appear more organized and professional. However, be sure to really listen to all questions and answer what is actually asked of you, rather than solely relying on what you have prepared for support materials.

DON'TS

1. Don't assume anything. Be sure all your assertions are backed up with generous amounts of research and documentation. For example, if the success of your business is contingent upon a market growth of 5 percent, be sure you can specify exactly when, why, and how that growth will occur, and be ready to provide the baseline from which you derived that figure. If you can't, your audience will likely see right through you, doubt your credibility, and begin to ask some extremely probing questions to challenge your understanding of the premises for your other business decisions.

2. Don't assume that your audience automatically knows as much or more than you in any given area. If you are presenting with a team, assign a nonspeaking member to scan faces in the audience for signs of confusion, disagreement, or overkill. That person can then subtly relay to you that your presentation needs to shift course to better meet the needs of your audience.

3. Don't forget the rightful place of slide material in presentations. You are not speaking to support material presented on your slides—just the opposite. If the audience members didn't want to hear from you, they could have simply requested an e-mailed set of slides (this sometimes happens, by the way). Sure, the slides look great, and you spent a lot of time on their design, but they don't hold the real power here—you do. So don't allocate more power to your slides than they warrant. Don't distribute copies of your slides beforehand—doing so gives your audience an excuse to look at paper copies versus the real thing. Also, feel free to skip a slide or make jumps in sequence if you suspect that the material, as prepared, is not the best fit for a particular audience.

4. Don't usurp your own intelligence. You know more about your business than anyone else in the room, so why make it appear otherwise by clinging to note cards while you speak? Have faith in your ability to remember what you need to, when you need to. If you absolutely cannot give up the note cards, at least save them for the far more detailed information that is likely to be conveyed in a Q&A session.

5. Don't use your slides as notes to remember what to say next. Putting down note cards sometimes triggers a tendency to speak with your back to members of your audience, and you "read" your slides. Please don't talk to the projection screen; it can't help you acquire funding. Sure, a quick glance here and there is fine, but keep in mind that this presentation is really a conversation with people who are deciding whether a partnership with you makes sense. To make that decision, they need to get to know you better, and it's hard to do that if you are not speaking directly to them.

6. Don't cram too much of anything onto a single slide. A shorter presentation time doesn't mean taking the same material and bundling it on fewer slides. Sometimes it's easier for audiences to understand complex concepts if they are broken across more slides with ample white space, rather than reduced to a single slide. What's most important is comprehension—sometimes that's better served by spending 10 seconds per three simple slides versus 30 seconds on a more complex one.

7. Don't simply read your slides—interpret them. Reading anything verbatim only works to put your audience to sleep. They're all capable readers—why do they need you to do that for them? Rather, use text bullet points as springboards to catapult you into new and interesting content areas for discussion.

8. Don't make your audience think too hard. If they need to work too hard to decipher your financial data or graphics, then they are more likely to tune out for the remainder of your presentation and therefore less likely to really pay attention to what you are saying. Also, leaving your audience members to interpret data on their own can be dangerous. They may draw conclusions that are inconsistent with your own.

You'll also build a lot of credibility with your audience if you can thoroughly walk them through the particulars of the way things work, and why, in your business. After all, no one should know that better than you, and you are demonstrating such.

NUMBER ONE—"EVERYONE THINKS MY IDEA IS CRAZY"

Anyone who has traveled by train or ship has seen them—the large rectangular cargo containers that are shipped throughout the world. Have you ever wondered what's inside? Typical guesses range from automobiles to home appliances, but certainly not people.

Unless you are Brian McCarthy. Having grown up in New Mexico, Brian visited Juarez, Mexico on a class trip while a student. What he saw there would change his life forever. Despite that more than 80 percent of the 300 border factories in Juarez are U.S.-owned, the ramshackle tin-and-cardboard shanties that crowd the landscape display indisputable evidence of vast poverty and disease. There are no household utilities, services, or security—yet this city draws a steady stream of refugees from even poorer regions of Mexico seeking factory work. Known as "the capital of murdered women," this city of 1.5 million is home to assembly plants, known as "maquiladoras," that are operated by companies such as General Electric and DuPont. More than 60 percent of maquiladora workers are women and girls, many as young as 13 or 14, who earn $55 a week.[2] And each year, hundreds are raped, murdered, or just disappear while traveling to and from work, or from their unsecured homes while they sleep.

Brian knew he wanted to help these less fortunate people, but he didn't know how to do so until the day he drove by a West Coast shipping port. "I saw all these shipping containers, piled 16 to 20 high, and the solution just hit me," says Brian. "Why not take these excess containers and remodel them into housing structures for the people of Juarez who have no homes."

Brian shared his idea with his cousin Pablo Nava, and their company "Por Fin Nuestra Casa" was born. Now an official LLC, licensed in Albuquerque, New Mexico, PFNC is constructing a two-wide–two-tall prototype, and developing relationships with many international organizations.

"Having roots in Mexico, I was immediately drawn to the idea, and together we began developing sketches, and further planning out the homes," explains Pablo. "Brian and I had talked about the business for hours and hours on the phone. We wrote down everything we knew, and everything we wanted to know."

Pablo credits the business plan writing process with helping to sharpen and mold their idea into a viable not-for-profit organization.

"The business plan forced us to get it all on paper, one step at a time. It was an amazing experience in that we really were forced to put our brains together and figure out what this was," explains Pablo. "The problem we had was in convincing people that this dark, murky container could be transformed into a beautiful home to live in."

Brian and Pablo say they have faced numerous obstacles since launching their business in 2007. A major difficulty is communicating with people who are unfamiliar with the living conditions in Juarez, as many can't understand why someone would want to live in a home that was once a shipping container.

"Belief is a major obstacle for us—it's very difficult for some people to have confidence in our business because it is such a radical idea," says Brian. "We knew that if we wanted people to understand the idea, we needed them to see what kind of living conditions these workers faced."

Unable to transport nonbelievers to Juarez to see for themselves what a vast improvement former shipping container homes would be over the miles of cardboard and tin shacks, Brian and Pablo instead created a computer-generated model and slide show of the transformed home, and a video of living conditions in Juarez. "We knew that if we wanted people to understand the idea, we needed them to see what kind of living conditions these workers faced."

The advice this team offers to would-be entrepreneurs speaks directly to the heart of this chapter—know your audience. "You may find that some people don't support the idea; not because it is a bad idea, but because you are not painting the right picture for them to see," explains Brian. "You'll learn that different people will like different things about what you want to do, and that you have to tailor how you speak to people who have different interests."

"If you really are passionate about your idea, and I mean really passionate about it," he continues, "then you will be rewarded somehow some way, and take away so much from the experience."

CONCLUSION

Presentations really are a lot of fun. The common denominator is content, but the variance in audience groups will require that each presentation be unique. Keep in mind that no one knows your business as well as you, and no one could possibly be more passionate about it. Don't be afraid to let go of your notes and go with the flow and energy in the room. Also, don't become defensive during Q&A sessions because the insights garnered during these discussions offer fresh and valuable perspectives from highly intelligent people. Keep an open mind, but don't lose sight of your dreams.

REVIEW

At least three distinct presentation opportunities are associated with new business development: the elevator pitch, the venture/business plan competition, and meetings with potential investors. Each presentation opportunity comes with a unique set of requirements for preparation and implementation, although common "do's and don'ts" exist for creating an effective presentation style.

ASSIGNMENTS

1. Develop three versions of an elevator pitch—one timed for 30 seconds, another for 1 minute, and a third for 3 minutes. Practice each pitch until the words flow comfortably and you are confident that you could deliver them any place at any time.

2. Identify competitions with criteria that you already have met or would likely be able to meet over the next 12 months. The lists within this chapter and at the end of this book will help you get started. Once you've determined deadlines for competition(s) for which you are eligible, build a work schedule "to-do" list backward from the date for initial submissions. Some competitions require participants to submit entire business plans, and others ask for only executive summaries at the preliminary stages. Developing a spreadsheet to show which documents are required by each competition on which dates is an approach that often proves helpful.

3. Conduct an Internet search to develop a list of venture capitalists with areas of specialization related to your new business. Use this research to learn all that you can about key partners, past funding success stories, and requirements to initiate a potential investment meeting opportunity.

ENDNOTES

1. www.sba.gov
2. "To Work and Die in Juarez," by Evelyn Nieves. Mother Jones Magazine. May/June 2002. http://www.motherjones.com/news/feature/2002/05/juarez.html

A *FLASH* SEATS

Sarah Coffman
Joshua Francis
Justin Carter
Radu A. Olievschi

CONTENTS

1. EXECUTIVE SUMMARY

Flash Seats is a system that maximizes revenues for sporting and entertainment venues and offers complete control of the secondary ticket market. This goal is achieved through complete elimination of physical tickets.

Flash Seats is protected by U.S. Patent # 6,496,809 B1 specifically for combining the paperless ticket notion with that of a virtual ticket exchange system. In essence, *Flash* Seats creates a virtual marketplace for the exchange of tickets, using the model of the stock market. Secondary buyers and sellers of tickets can trade tickets at any moment, in a virtual marketplace, taking direct advantage of price fluctuations.

Flash Seats offers unique benefits to venues and teams by increasing revenues through trading in the virtual marketplace (a commission is charged to ticket traders, each time a ticket is traded) and by reducing costs (e.g., printing and distribution of traditional tickets). *Flash* Seats also has a unique set of offerings for ticket holders. It provides a legal, secure, and profitable medium to exchange tickets and it allows for an easy transfer of tickets.

With regard to the legality of *Flash* Seats' operations, it does not infringe on any present regulation. Current laws were written to protect the monopoly status of ticket sellers and to maintain a safe environment at the points of entry to the venues. *Flash* Seats directly fortifies the intent of the law since, through its patented marketplace, it protects the venues' ticket ownership rights.

Flash Seats benefits from three revenue streams: (1) software licenses awarded to venues, (2) trading commissions for the tickets exchanged, and (3) software maintenance charges. The patented system utilizes existing technologies and practices that have already been proven successful in other industries, such as electronic tickets for the airline industry and online stock trading for the stock market.

The industry that *Flash* Seats will penetrate is currently characterized by dispersion among competitors and few barriers to entry. The three main types of venues *Flash* Seats targets are collegiate athletic venues (teams), professional sporting venues (teams), and entertainment venues.

Flash Seats will show increasing profits throughout the first five years of operations. The break-even point is reached in Year 2. Throughout Year 3 and Year 4, net profits rise to $0.9 million and $2 million, respectively. In Year 5, as the first customers become fully integrated into the *Flash* Seats virtual marketplace, profits soar to $6 million. All figures represent profits after tax.

Flash Seats Corp. will be managed by a team headed by Brett Nakfoor, the creator of the patented *Flash* Seats technology. The management team of the corporation consists of individuals whose experiences directly address the key aspects involved in the patented virtual marketplace. The members' backgrounds combine the following skills: commodities trading, software sales, credit/debit management, strategic analysis, high-tech industry operations, international trade, special events management, performing arts management, and public relations.

1.1. OBJECTIVES

Flash **Seats** represents an innovative system that gives control of the secondary market and maximizes revenues for sporting and entertainment venues. As such, the main objectives of Flash Seats Corp. in order to implement and market its virtual marketplace are as follows:

- Conduct beta-testing of the *Flash* **Seats** virtual marketplace, using 2% to 5% of a venue's tickets, within the first six to eight months;
- Complete the full system development and its beta-testing within one year;
- Penetrate market and acquire two additional professional sporting venues as customers every year;
- Convert each professional venue entirely to *Flash* **Seats** paperless system within four years.

1.2. MISSION

Flash **Seats** will revolutionize the ticketing industry by restoring control of the secondary market to sporting and entertainment venues, and facilitating the distribution and exchange of tickets to improve profitability.

1.3. KEYS TO SUCCESS

The success of the *Flash* **Seats** virtual marketplace depends upon several major elements that are outlined in the current section. A more detailed description of the concrete measures to be implemented and a corresponding timeline are presented in section 4.0 of this plan.

The keys to success are as follows:

- Obtain first round of financing in the amount of $1.2 million;
- Implement successful beta-testing and full system development within one year;
- Conduct negotiations and sign first customer (venue) by the end of the first year of operation;
- Maintain a steady increase in the customer base, by adding two additional customers per year during the first two years of operation.

2. PATENT AND CONCEPT OVERVIEW

Flash **Seats** is a system that maximizes revenues for sporting and entertainment venues and offers complete control of the secondary ticket market. This goal is achieved through complete elimination of physical tickets. Access to venues on the dates of events is done using a magnetic stripe card system or a personal identification code that matches the buyer with his/her virtual tickets stored electronically on a server.

Flash **Seats** is protected by U.S. Patent # 6,496,809 B1 specifically for combining the paperless ticket notion with that of a virtual ticket exchange system. In essence, *Flash* **Seats** creates a virtual marketplace for the exchange of tickets, using the model of the stock market. Secondary buyers and sellers of tickets can trade tickets at any moment taking direct advantage of price fluctuations. The medium for the exchange of tickets is a controlled virtual marketplace where buyers and seller can log in and be guaranteed secured transactions, complete confidentiality, and utter legality regarding the trading of their tickets.

The patented *Flash* **Seats** system has two primary features:

1. *Virtual marketplace based on stock-market model.* ***Flash*** **Seats** creates a centralized secondary market similar to the NASDAQ stock market. The patented ***Flash*** **Seats** platform is fundamentally different from online auctions (e.g., *eBay*) because it offers complete price fluidity, a higher probability for fans to purchase a ticket at any time, and full and accurate disclosure of information regarding supply and demand of tickets.

2. *Paperless tickets.* Paperless tickets are held electronically in a database and matched with their owners at the venue gate. Since each ticket is held in paperless form until it is used to enter a venue, tickets can be instantly transferred from buyer to seller in real time. Although no tickets can be printed from a desktop, kiosk, or anywhere else outside of the venue itself, the paperless tickets can be traded on the virtual marketplace an infinite number of times, from different sellers to different buyers.

FLASH SEATS BENEFITS TO VENUES AND TEAMS

- *Increased revenues through trading on virtual marketplace.* A commission is charged to both the buyer and the seller of a ticket each time a ticket is traded. As tickets can trade an unlimited number of times, a new and significant revenue stream is created for the venue. The virtual marketplace will draw revenues both from ticket holders who otherwise would trade their tickets on the "uncontrolled" secondary market, and from ticket holders who would not trade their tickets in the absence of a reliable and easy to use marketplace, like the one ***Flash*** **Seats** creates.
- *Control of the secondary market.* The absence of the physical ticket eliminates the possibility of any secondary market trading without the venue's knowledge or consent.
- *Reduced costs.* Through the patented ***Flash*** **Seats** system, paper ticket printing and distribution costs are eliminated.
- *Improves ticketing information.* Data on customers, supply and demand of tickets, current ticket value for various events, and so on is gathered by monitoring the controlled virtual marketplace.

FLASH SEATS BENEFITS TO TICKET HOLDERS

- *A legal, secure, and profitable medium to exchange tickets.* ***Flash*** **Seats** offers ticket holders the possibility to trade their tickets in a reliable and easy to use fashion.
- *Ease of transfer.* Tickets can be transferred to buyers or friends and family through the ***Flash*** **Seats** virtual marketplace quickly and easily.

TECHNOLOGY CONSIDERATIONS

Flash **Seats** will be sold directly to venues. No association with other ticketing services providers (e.g., *Paciolan*, *Ticketmaster*) will be made prior to installation of the system.

With regard to the initial sale of tickets (e.g., before any secondary exchanges occurs), *Flash* **Seats** can work hand-in-hand with other ticket allocation systems that venues may already have in function. Specifically, *Flash* **Seats** imports information from the ticket allocation systems already in place and then facilitates the virtual exchange of tickets in a controlled virtual marketplace. Software running the entire operation will link the various servers facilitating the marketplace and the retrieval of ticket ownership information. Flash Seats Corp. will offer support to train venue employees and a call center will be established so venues and ticket holders can receive additional help.

REVENUE SOURCES FOR *FLASH* SEATS CORP.

Revenues for both the venue initially selling its tickets and for Flash Seats Corp. are created by charging a commission for every transaction involving the exchange of a ticket on the virtual marketplace. More precisely, a commission is perceived as a percentage of the trading price of every ticket. Revenues are generated both when tickets trade at increasing prices as well as when they trade at decreasing values. Specific information regarding the financial aspects of the operation is detailed in section 8.0 of the plan.

Flash Seats benefits from three revenue streams:

- Software licenses awarded to venues. This fee will cover the installation of the hardware and integration of the software required with the existing ticketing system at the venue.
- Trading commissions for the tickets exchanged, as described above.
- Software maintenance charges.

* A functional diagram of the entire *Flash* Seats system is included in Appendix A.

---

3. MARKET ANALYSIS SUMMARY

After explaining the specific services that *Flash* Seats offers, it is useful to describe the overview of the market that the patented system will penetrate.

Currently, the sports and entertainment ticketing industry has not reached maturity. It is characterized by dispersion among services offered and ongoing search for solutions to improve existing processes. There are two large service providers involved in the initial selling and distribution of tickets, and thousands of ticket brokers in the secondary market. All are extensively using the Internet to conduct operations, although they also employ calling centers and physical locations. Despite the introduction of print-at-home tickets, which was seen as a serious process improvement, presently no company has considered completely eliminating paper tickets. *Flash* Seats will fill in this gap and identify additional sources of revenue by empowering the venues to profit from all of their ticket sales. This eliminates secondary brokers.

When considering the ticketing industry, the name *Ticketmaster* invariably comes to mind. In 2002 it reached overall sales of over \$4 billion.[1] Beginning in September 2003, the company has become involved in the secondary market by implementing an auction system.[2] However, because this system does not eliminate paper tickets, it does not address the needs that the patented *Flash* Seats technology does.

Rather than compete with *Ticketmaster*, *Flash* Seats will tackle secondary ticket brokers who do not pose a strong competitive threat due to their degree of dispersion. There are no major secondary ticket brokers that are consolidated into operations comparable to *Ticketmaster*'s size and strength. By contrast, there are thousands of independent brokers. They create a secondary ticket exchange market that resembles a "black market" whose size—although difficult to determine in dollar terms—is estimated as being quite large since the independent brokers are so numerous.

In an effort to capture some of the benefits of secondary ticket exchanges, teams and venues are constantly trying to dissuade the excessive trading of their tickets, by employing laws and other restrictions (e.g., the team at University of Notre Dame revokes season ticket privileges if scalping is proven). Similarly there are various laws that attempt to curtail scalping with more or less success. This topic and the legality of *Flash* Seats are further explained in section 7.0.

Recognizing and addressing such issues, *Flash* Seats will directly target sports and entertainment venues, as well as sports teams.

3.1. MARKET SEGMENTATION

In bringing the patented *Flash* **Seats** to the market, three different groups will be targeted: college athletics, professional athletics, and entertainment venues. The overall size of the market was estimated in 2000 as follows:

- $9.8 billion for entertainment venues (e.g., theatre, opera);
- $9.3 billion for spectator sports;[3]

The remaining portion of this section explains the three main target groups for *Flash* **Seats**:

Collegiate athletics are characterized by a rather reduced interest in profit maximization. Instead, they are far more sensitive to control of tickets and image issues. The schools obtain a large part of their funds through donations. In turn, many collegiate athletic venues deem ticket allocation as a means of rewarding alumni and students. Consequently, these venues are interested in maintaining control of who attends their athletic events and in ensuring that nobody earns a dishonest profit from selling their tickets on the secondary market. Finally, most universities and colleges sell season tickets and regular tickets mainly to students, alumni, and donors. *Flash* **Seats** effectively responds to these needs by eliminating paper tickets and thus making obsolete the very object of illegal trading. Concomitantly, *Flash* **Seats** provides ticket holders with the possibility to legally exchange their tickets in a virtual medium that is directly overseen by the collegiate venue.

Professional athletics refers mainly to the big four sports: football, basketball, baseball, and hockey. These customers represent a very different picture from the collegiate venues. They are primarily profit driven, they often operate large or expanding stadiums, and they deal with teams that are strapped for cash. For very popular events, tickets are resold numerous times and change many hands without the venues (teams) receiving any of the proceeds. Over half of the tickets sold by the National Basketball Association (NBA) and the National Hockey League (NHL) are season tickets and many of the fans simply cannot attend all of the 41–45 scheduled games. In addition, some venues have been funded through local taxes and because of this, the public often feels that it has a right to attend the games. For this reason, prices are often kept low, at a value far below the real, market value of the tickets. *Flash* **Seats** directly solves these issues by not interfering with the initial low prices of tickets and by offering the controlled medium of exchange that captures the additional cash inflow generated by ticket trading at true market values. Until now, such additional sources of revenue have remained in the hands of secondary ticket brokers. Through its innovative, patented approach, *Flash* **Seats** would return these revenues to venues and teams.

Entertainment venues includes two main areas: (1) popular music concerts and (2) musicals, other plays, variety entertainment and so on. Much like in the case of popular sporting events, tickets to well-known entertainment happenings sell in a matter of hours or even minutes after they are initially put on sale. Artists and venues are interested in reporting that a particular event is soldout much in advance. However, this affects profit maximization, because the prices charged do not necessarily reflect the value that the public is willing to attribute to the tickets. This gap in profitability is filled by secondary ticket brokers, many of whom guarantee very good seats to practically any entertainment event, up until a few hours before the event takes place. Waiting lists for interested spectators and prices easily reaching several thousands of dollars for only two seats are commonplace. *Flash* **Seats** directly transforms these cash flows into revenue sources for venues and artists. The controlled ticket exchange can still guarantee last-minute seats, but for each transaction the venue registers a percentage revenue.

The ensuing sections detail the targeting techniques that Flash Seats Corp. will employ in order to clearly present its patented technology and its advantages to these three types of customers.

3.2. TARGET MARKET SEGMENT STRATEGY

As the financial analysis in section 8.0 will demonstrate, for the ***Flash* Seats** marketplace to be appealing, it must be employed by frequently sold-out venues. Concurrently, due to the manner in which revenues are generated for Flash Seats Corp.—commission fees charged on every ticket exchanged—it follows that larger, sold-out venues and teams that play more frequently are more profitable.

The following paragraphs describe the strategies for addressing the needs of the main customers identified in the previous section.

Collegiate athletics are appealing because of their size and loyal fan base. In addition, if a collegiate athletic department decided to use ***Flash* Seats**, the virtual marketplace would be employed for various sports at once (e.g., football and basketball). In other words, one sale to a collegiate venue would yield multiple returns. In addition to this, many collegiate athletic venues are characterized by older—sometimes antiquated—technological systems. *Scantron* forms and ticket mailings are not unusual. Therefore, such venues are interested in innovative new systems that can readily answer all of their needs, rather than invest in new technologies that only solve some of the problems. (The famous Notre Dame stadium could provide an excellent point to start the ***Flash* Seats** marketplace and demonstrate its benefits.)

Professional athletics—such as Major League Baseball (MLB) and NBA—provide an excellent base for the ***Flash* Seats** marketplace due to the large number of games per season and the size of stadiums. This large number of events combined with the large number of spectators guarantee considerable cash flows from secondary ticket exchanges. Over 50 percent of tickets sold represents season tickets, indicating a stable base of customers. It also indicates, as mentioned before, that ticket buyers may simply not be able to use all of their season tickets, in which case they would benefit from an organized medium of ticket trading. As opposed to collegiate sporting events, professional ones are constantly interested in profit maximization. Through its innovative, patented approach, ***Flash* Seats** offers a means to capture secondary market dollars and enhance profitability. Finally, in the case of MLB and NBA, the two sport seasons complement each other, allowing for a positive cash flow year round for Flash Seats Corp.

Entertainment venues often operate all throughout the calendar year and make up for the smaller size of some of the locations (e.g., Broadway theatre houses) through the large number of performances. The undeniable popularity of certain musical acts (e.g., Beyoncé Knowles' *Ladies' First Tour*, Cher's *Farewell Tour*), certain theatrical plays (e.g., *The Producers*, **Miss Saigon**) and certain variety shows (e.g., Celine Dion's *A New Day*, Cirque du Soleil's *Zumanity*) affords an extensive number of secondary ticket exchanges. In addition to this, entertainment events have a particular advantage over sporting events in that their popularity often covers a wider geographical area. The customer base for certain Las Vegas or Broadway acts, for example, comprises the entire U.S. territory and often extends beyond the country's borders. This has the potential to increase secondary ticket exchanges considerably. Given this context, ***Flash* Seats** would decidedly maximize profits for venues.

3.3. SERVICE BUSINESS ANALYSIS

This section of the plan investigates the particular aspects of the competitive forces in the ticketing industry. First of all, it should be noted that there are two types of competitors:

1. Third-party ticket sellers;

2. Secondary market ticket vendors (ticket brokers).

Despite this apparently clear-cut delineation, the operations of some of the major companies conducting business in this industry overlap as they often attempt to cover both areas noted above.

By far the strongest players in the first category of competitors are *Ticketmaster* and *Paciolan.*

Nothing short of a phenomenon in the short-lived history of Internet ticketing to date, *Ticketmaster* is either admired as the epitome of success in the industry or detested for allegedly having a monopoly. In both cases, its strength remains undisputed. Yet in reality, it only controls 10 percent of all third-party ticket sales,[4] indicating that the realm of ticket vendors is highly fragmented. Currently, *Ticketmaster* is involved in developing an online auction system that would be sanctioned by teams (venues), would be based on print-at-home tickets, and that would be reliable for fans because it would guarantee authenticity.[5] As will be explained in section 4.0, the patented *Flash* **Seats** has a different approach to trading tickets that is more flexible, secure, and profitable.

Paciolan is mainly focused on college athletics. Instead of taking over ticket sales—like *Ticketmaster*—it offers complete software services to colleges and universities, allowing them to manage their own ticketing systems.[6] *Paciolan*, too, is currently proposing a small-scale virtual auction platform that is being used at Ohio State University.[7] As opposed to this, *Flash* **Seats** is focused on an entirely paperless ticket, whose benefits are further described in section 4.0.

The second category of *Flash* **Seats** competitors are the secondary market ticket *brokers*. Their competitive strength is not as pronounced due to the fact that they are scattered both geographically and in terms of type of events targeted, size of operations, and so on. Secondary market ticket brokers purchase and resell tickets at a premium price. They provide a medium for the resale of tickets. Despite their decentralization, there are attempts to consolidate various secondary ticket brokers. The United States Ticket Broker Association (USTBA) unites over 150 ticket brokers who sell tickets collectively and abide by the same code of ethics.[8] *Onlinetickets.com* is another such example. The company represents 22 different brokers and hoped to have 6,000 to 8,000 tickets listed by the third quarter of 2002.[9]

3.3.1. COMPETITION AND BUYING PATTERNS

Faced with a variety of choices for selling their tickets, teams and venues are mostly interested in the aspect of reliability. They have a strong preference for a trustworthy system that can efficiently handle all of their ticketing needs without incurring any malfunction that would shake the patrons' confidence in the team or venue. In fact, many collegiate athletic venues refuse to switch to more advanced ticketing platforms for fear of breakdowns caused by unreliable systems. The manner in which *Flash* **Seats** responds to these concerns is detailed in the following section presenting its competitive edge.

4. STRATEGY AND IMPLEMENTATION SUMMARY

This fourth section of the plan details the strategy for developing and marketing *Flash* **Seats** to sports and entertainment venues.

4.1. COMPETITIVE EDGE

As opposed to *Ticketmaster*, *Paciolan*, and the host of hundreds of secondary ticket brokers, **Flash Seats** provides a unique offering by directly addressing the problem of ticket scalping and therefore generating maximum revenues for venues and teams. More specifically, the patented marketplace *Flash* **Seats** features the following competitive advantages:

- **Maximizes revenues** by creating a controlled medium (e.g., marketplace) for secondary ticket trading;
- **Maximizes control** that venues (teams) have over their tickets. By eliminating physical (e.g., paper) tickets, *Flash* **Seats** ensures that no ticket exchanges can occur outside the controlled virtual marketplace;

- **Improves venues' (teams') image** by offering fans a legal, secure, and profitable medium to exchange tickets;
- **Improves flow of information** for venues (e.g., data on customers, supply and demand, etc.) by monitoring the controlled virtual marketplace.

Ultimately, *Flash* **Seats** improves the relationship between venues and their fans, because it offers ticket buyers the best of both worlds. Those interested in cheaper tickets can still obtain them directly from the venues, whereas the ones willing to pay a premium for good seats can do so, using the *Flash* **Seats** marketplace.

In addition to these unique offerings, *Flash* **Seats** is protected by a U.S. Patent (U.S. Patent # 6,496,809 B1) for combining the paperless ticket notion with that of a virtual ticket exchange system. The *Flash* **Seats** platform uses technologies that have already been proven successful in other markets. Therefore, the sole remaining step is the combination of the following elements:

- Magnetic card swipes (turnstiles) to ensure access to venues on event days;
- Venue ticket databases holding ticket ownership information;
- Internet database/exchange allowing for exchange of tickets.

Finally, it should be fully explained that *Flash* **Seats'** uniqueness is the combination of a controlled marketplace with the notion of paperless tickets. When secondary market ticket exchanges occur, they can only take place on the *Flash* **Seats** marketplace because there are no physical tickets. Issues such as buyer/seller privacy, legality, and reliability of transactions are built into the *Flash* **Seats** virtual marketplace. Concomitantly, the patented *Flash* **Seats** platform is fundamentally different from online auctions such as the ones endorsed by *eBay*. *Flash* **Seats** is designed on the model of the stock market. As such, it offers:

- Complete price fluidity—buyers and sellers know exactly what the most recent price level is;
- A higher probability for fans to purchase a ticket at any time—not only when someone happens to be auctioning one;
- Full and accurate disclosure of information regarding supply and demand—such as the value that buyers attach to a certain event.

4.2. MILESTONES

Following the description of *Flash* **Seats'** competitive advantages, the current section fully explains the development of the system and of its needed components. A timeline is presented, following *Flash* **Seats** from idea to fully developed and used system.

The success of *Flash* **Seats** depends upon several elements that need to be created as follows:

- Working Demonstration Platform—to conduct preliminary functionality tests;
- Web Site Design and Hosting—to educate customers and ticket buyers about how *Flash* **Seats** operates and the advantages it has to offer;
- Technical Architecture Design:
    - Enhanced Web site—to expand initial Web site to fully functional interactive status and allow for data storage;
    - Development of Exchange—to construct the controlled virtual marketplace inspired by the stock market, using the Working Demo Platform;
    - Development of Total Solution—to integrate all developed components through API (Application Programming Interface);
- Beta-Testing—to conduct final functionality tests;
- Call Center—to serve as assistance to both venues (teams) and ticket buyers and sellers;
- Build Out at Venues—to put in place system components at various venues.

The above elements have been estimated to occur at the dates approximated in the timeline below:

- **May 2004**: Technical architecture design.
- **June 2004**: Acquire site for beta-testing.
- **September 2004**: Conduct beta-testing. Negotiate contract with a MLB team.
- **February 2005**: Conduct preliminary tests with MLB team. Negotiate contract with a NBA team.
- **April 2005**: Begin operations with first major customer—MLB team.
- **August 2005**: Conduct preliminary tests with NBA team.
- **November 2005**: Begin operations with second major customer—NBA team.

The above timeline can be represented graphically as follows:

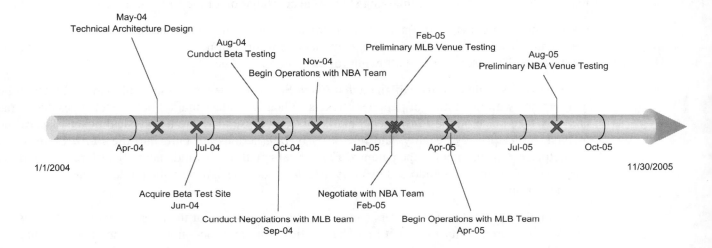

The following sections expand on the strategy employed to effectively market *Flash* **Seats**.

4.3. MARKETING STRATEGY

The following two sections detail the marketing and sales strategies to bring *Flash* **Seats** to its potential customers.

Given the nature of the services offered by *Flash* **Seats** (i.e. a virtual ticket exchange system), the marketing strategy used will parallel a model that is often employed in the software industry, that of selling a product or service before it exists or while it is being developed. The rationale behind this notion is that the final service does not have a physical nature and therefore what is being sold consists of "vision and value." Given this context, the marketing strategy depends heavily on the creation of a clear value proposition. As a result of this, and considering the novelty of the idea behind *Flash* **Seats**, the selling efforts should be concurrent with the development of the product.

More specifically, the sales force will use PowerPoint presentations, technical documents, and online demos to prove what *Flash* **Seats** consists of and has to offer. A key idea is the constant underlining that *Flash* **Seats** utilizes existing technologies and practices that have already been proven successful in other industries. Electronic tickets have been so popular in the airline industry that today companies like American Airlines sell 85 percent of their tickets in that format.[10] Similarly, online stock trading and retail are both multibillion dollar industries. *Flash* **Seats**' controlled virtual ticket exchange will be hosted by ***Truequote.com***, a company that has been around for 10 years.[11] Finally, the process of electronic reading of various cards with magnetic strips has been widely used for the past 20 years. Essentially, *Flash* **Seats** does not reinvent any wheels with regard to the components it uses. It only combines them in a pioneering fashion.

4.4. SALES STRATEGY

The marketing concepts explained in the previous section translate into several selling tactics to be employed for **Flash** Seats. The resulting sales strategy is the object of the current section.

For beta testing, one venue will be targeted. **Flash** Seats will be sold by offering free installation and the proposition that only a small percentage of all tickets will be included in the **Flash** Seats system. **Flash** Seats and the original ticket allocation and distribution system used by the venue will coexist for a limited period, until the benefits and reliability that **Flash** Seats offers become obvious.

Consequently, negotiations will be conducted with MLB teams. Individual venues and teams will be targeted directly. The same strategy of gradual introduction of **Flash** Seats alongside the existing ticket allocation and distribution system will be used. As momentum is gained, **Flash** Seats will eventually evolve into the single platform used by teams (venues) to sell all of their tickets. To balance the cash flows throughout the year, NBA and NHL teams will be signed on next. Ultimately, entertainment venues will be targeted using data collected as a selling point.

Before concluding, a few major observations should be made with regard to the sales strategy. First, as the financial analysis in section 8.0 will demonstrate, for **Flash** Seats to be profitable, it must be employed by frequently sold-out venues. For similar reasons, larger sold-out venues that host events more often are more profitable. Second, **Flash** Seats can be tailored to meet the different needs of every venue. It can easily be integrated with the existing ticketing system used by a particular venue. Moreover, different types of venues may have different types of needs. Collegiate venues, for example, are more interested in control over their tickets, whereas professional venues pursue profit maximization. As demonstrated in section 4.1, **Flash** Seats effectively addresses all of these needs.

4.4.1. SALES FORECAST
The table that follows details the dollar figures related to the forecast sale of **Flash** Seats:

- Trading commissions refer to revenues generated from all ticket exchanges;
- Software licensing refers to the fee paid by venues to gain access to the **Flash** Seats marketplace;
- Maintenance refers to fees for software upgrades and upkeep;
- Advertising refers to revenues generated from advertising on **Flash** Seats Web site;
- Money transfer fees refer to fees paid by Flash Seats Corp. to Visa/PayPal for accepting and distributing funds.

The breakdown of the figures in the table is as follows:

Year 1: System development and beta-testing. No sales revenue.
Year 2: Figures based on two customers as follows:

MLB Team generating the following types of revenues:
    Trading commissions
    Software licensing
    Software maintenance

The revenue model assumes gradual deployment of the **Flash** Seats system, starting with 2,000 paperless tickets and working up to 4,000 seats in the second half of the season. Each of the 32 MLB venues has a capacity of 35,000 to 40,000 seats. These venues will use a progressive model to implement the transition to paperless tickets. This creates a high potential for future revenues as more paperless tickets replace traditional paper tickets.

NBA Team generating the following types of revenues:
    Trade commissions
    Software licensing
    Software maintenance

This revenue model also assumes gradual deployment of the *Flash* **Seats** system, starting with 2,000 paperless tickets and working up to 4,000 seats in the second half of the season. Each of the 29 NBA venues has a capacity of 15,000 to 20,000 seats. These venues will use a progressive model to implement the transition to paperless tickets. This creates a high potential for future revenues as more paperless tickets replace traditional paper tickets.

Note: Commission revenue in the table was generated as per the "Revenue metrics baseline," which succumbs to the 8.1 Assumptions for the revenue model

Year 3: Figures based on two customers as follows:

One new MLB team is added, generating the following types of revenues (like above):
Trading commissions
Software licensing
Software maintenance

The revenue model for this new team is identical to the model described above.

Following the assumption explained above, the first MLB team uses 6,000 paperless tickets during the first-half of the season and 8,000 paperless tickets during the second-half of the season. Similarly, the NBA team expands to 6,000 paperless tickets by the end of the second season

Year 4: Figures based on three customers (2 MLB teams and 1 NBA team) following the increasing rate of paperless ticket usage described before.

Year 5: Figures based on three customers (2 MLB teams and 1 NBA team), following the increasing rate of paperless ticket usage described before. The first customer (the MLB team) starts using paperless tickets exclusively causing revenues to increase substantially.

Exact figures follow in the table below:

Sales Forecast					
Sales	FY 2005	FY 2006	FY 2007	FY 2008	FY 2009
Trading Commissions (in dollars)	0	797,475	2,232,930	4,106,996	11,045,029
Software Licenses (in dollars)	0	47,368	148,026	274,342	623,684
Software Maintenance (in dollars)	0	1,579	4,934	9,145	20,789
Advertising (in dollars)	0	24,000	48,000	72,000	96,000
Total Sales (in dollars)	**0**	**870,422**	**2,433,891**	**4,462,483**	**11,785,502**
Direct Cost of Sales	FY 2005	FY 2006	FY 2007	FY 2008	FY 2009
Money Transfer Fees (in dollars)	0	179,432	502,409	924,074	2,485,131
Subtotal Direct Cost of Sales (in dollars)	**0**	**179,432**	**502,409**	**924,074**	**2,485,131**

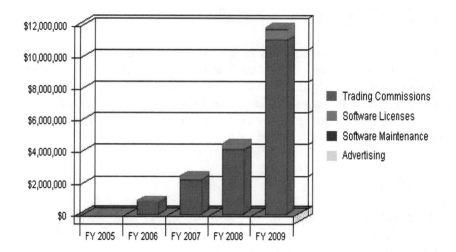

The graph shows sales for the first five years of operations. There are no sales during the first year due to the development of the system. During the second year there are sales of $800,000. Throughout Year 3 and Year 4, sales rise to $2.2 million and $4.1 million, respectively. In Year 5, the first MLB team customer becomes fully integrated into the *Flash* Seats system and this causes the large growth in sales from the periods before. Sales in Year 5 are $11 million.

4.5. EXIT STRATEGY

Ticketmaster and *Paciolan* both represent very large companies with strong interests in the ticketing industry. Due to the novelty of the patented *Flash* Seats marketplace, the success of the system will draw competitive pressures and potential offers to buy Flash Seats Corp. along with its patented system. When the major stakeholders in the corporation determine that potential offers made on *Flash* Seats are adequate, the company could be sold for a sum that would effectively compensate the stakeholders.

5. COMPANY SUMMARY

The current section details the ownership of the idea behind *Flash* Seats and the start-up costs inherent in the full development of this idea into a business operation.

5.1. COMPANY OWNERSHIP

Flash Seats is an original idea created by Brett Nakfoor that will be developed into a lucrative business operation as detailed in this plan. Currently, "Flash Seats" is registered as a for-profit C corporation in the state of California.

Brett Nakfoor is the only shareholder at the moment. The newly formed corporation will hold the patent for *Flash* Seats, will develop the virtual marketplace, and will sell the system directly to venues.

Brett Nakfoor will act as CEO of the newly formed company. The specific description of management positions within the company and of the management team are further described in section 6.0 of this business plan.

6. MANAGEMENT SUMMARY

Since the corporation behind *Flash* **Seats** is a start-up company, its management and personnel needs are not traditional ones. Brett Nakfoor, the owner of the idea behind Flash Seats will play a key role in the company. In addition, as few people as possible will be hired and the noncritical functions will be outsourced. As in many start-up companies, the employees will perform various tasks and will serve numerous roles simultaneously. As the following section will demonstrate, there is not a large need for personnel.

6.1. MANAGEMENT TEAM

Brett Nakfoor As creator of the patented idea of *Flash* **Seats**, Brett Nakfoor will play an instrumental role in the development of the virtual marketplace. His background is indicative of his experience in the fields covered by the various technologies that *Flash* **Seats** combines.

A University of Pennsylvania graduate with a major in Finance, Brett Nakfoor has worked for eight years as an Independent Floor Trader at the Chicago Mercantile Exchange (CME), the world's second largest futures exchange. During that time, he traded LIBOR, Eurodollar, S&P, and Foreign Currency futures and options.

For the following four years he worked for *i2 Technologies*, an enterprise software vendor that specializes in supply chain management. This afforded Mr. Nakfoor a detailed perspective on the marketing of software systems.

Currently, Brett Nakfoor is Regional Vice President for the Western United States at Money Network, a firm that specializes in pay cards in the debit and credit industry. He is in charge of sales teams, and all direct and channel sales.

Mr. Nakfoor's background extends over three main areas: (1) commodities trading, (2) software sales, and (3) credit/debit management. These also represent the three main functional aspects of *Flash* **Seats**.

Sarah Coffman Sarah Coffman's background combines a University of Notre Dame MBA in Entrepreneurship with a bachelor's degree in Recreation Management, both of which represent focal points in the development of *Flash* **Seats**. She has had extensive experience with large special events, including the Indian State Fair and Miami-Dade County Youth Fair. Her responsibilities have included establishing and maintaining relationships with fair directors and suppliers.

Josh Francis With a University of Notre Dame MBA in Corporate Strategy and a bachelor's degree in Applied Physics, Josh Francis blends the intricacies of strategic analysis with distinctive quantitative skills. One of his most important assets with regard to *Flash* **Seats** is represented by three years of experience with the Marriott Center Ticket Office, where he gained insights into the ticketing industry. He has also taught corporate strategy at *Continental Tire*, working directly with the management team.

Justin Carter Addressing many of *Flash* **Seats**' technical issues, Justin Carter's background is distinguished by his University of Notre Dame MBA in Finance and his bachelor's degree in Mechanical Engineering. His credentials include work experience in the high-tech industry and in international trade.

Radu Olievschi With a University of Notre Dame MBA in Marketing and a bachelor's degree in international business and performing arts, Radu Olievschi has worked in performing arts management, overseeing various projects. He has been directly involved in marketing campaigns for artistic events, public relations activities, and ticket pricing decision making.

* Complete resumes for the management team can be found in Appendix B.

6.2. PERSONNEL PLAN

This section describes the key positions needed to develop and market *Flash* **Seats**. The chart that follows represents the payroll needs for the positions at Flash Seats Corp.

Chief Executive Officer (CEO) - will manage the entire company. Duties will include strategic issues such as monitoring industry trends, the financial management of the company, and the direction of future business operations. The CEO will also act as a salesperson, energetically identifying potential customers and contributing to persuading them of the benefits that *Flash* Seats offers.

Vice President of Sales - will serve to oversee the company's sales efforts. The main duties of this position include a pronounced direct relationship with the venues (teams) using or interested in using *Flash* Seats, the development of marketing strategies and of all promotional materials, and the general overseeing of all marketing operations. The sales force of the company will be expanded as more customers are added.

Chief Technical Officer (CTO) - will coordinate the effective combination of all technologies that *Flash* Seats needs. This job calls for a person with the necessary technical skills to implement the connections between the controlled virtual marketplace, the technologies used by venues to allocate tickets and admit spectators on the dates of events, and other such components of the system. The CTO has the duty to oversee the entire architecture of *Flash* Seats. It is this person who makes most outsourcing decisions, draws technical documents, installs hardware and software elements on site at the venues (using outsourced labor), and provides technical data for the presentations needed by the VP of Sales and the CEO.

Exact payroll figures follow in the table below:

Personnel Plan					
	FY 2005	FY 2006	FY 2007	FY 2008	FY 2009
Chief Executive Officer (in dollars)	120,000	120,000	120,000	120,000	120,000
Vice President Sales (in dollars)	120,000	120,000	120,000	120,000	120,000
Chief Technology Officer (in dollars)	60,000	96,000	96,000	96,000	96,000
IT Personnel (in dollars)	0	72,000	72,000	72,000	72,000
IT Director (in dollars)	0	0	0	60,000	60,000
Total People	3	4	4	5	5
Total Payroll (in dollars)	**300,000**	**408,000**	**408,000**	**468,000**	**468,000**

7. LEGAL IMPLICATIONS REGARDING *FLASH* SEATS

Given that *Flash* Seats, through its patented technology, directly facilitates ticket trading, several legal issues come into play. First, a few definitions regarding tickets are in order:

According to Merriam-Webster's Dictionary of Law (1996),

- Face value refers to "the value indicated on the face of something (as a stock certificate)";
- Scalping means "(1) to buy and sell so as to make small quick profits; (2) to resell at greatly increased prices to profit by slight market fluctuations."

Presently, across the United States, ticket scalping laws are in place in some states, but enforcing them is difficult. Moreover, the legal environment is rapidly changing with regard to this topic, as laws fluctuate to keep up with technological innovations facilitating ticket trading.

Current laws were written to protect the monopoly status of ticket sellers and to maintain a safe environment at the points of entry to the venues. *Flash* **Seats** directly fortifies the intent of the law since, through its patented marketplace, it protects the venues' ticket ownership rights.

At least two other legal considerations directly pertain to *Flash* **Seats**. First, given the paperless tickets on which the patented *Flash* **Seats** marketplace is based, the issue of face value does not necessarily apply, since this value is not indicated in a tangible form. Second, *Flash* **Seats** could rely on the model used by *eBay* to circumvent legal difficulties. The well-known auction site restricts ticket trading based on where a particular venue is located, not where the ticket traders are found.[12]

Ultimately, the ongoing practices of other industry players are a clear indication of the legality of virtual ticket trading. Several recent cases have gone to trial involving the way in which the Internet is changing the face of the ticketing world. However, in none of these cases have the ticket trading facilitators, like *Flash* **Seats**, been implicated in breaking the law.[13]

Further in-depth analyses regarding the legal environment will be needed at the time *Flash* **Seats** becomes fully operational. Different laws will most likely apply to the location of various venues that *Flash* **Seats** serves.

8. FINANCIAL PLAN

The current section presents the most significant financial data pertaining to *Flash* **Seats**.

Flash Seats Corp. is expected to develop the *Flash* **Seats** system during the first year. Funding will be required for product development, during this first year, in an amount of $1,200,000. Currently Flash Seats Corp. is seeking investors to provide the first year development expenses.

Once the system is fully developed and cooperation with venues begins, the company's growth will be funded by the positive cash flow generated by the first two venues to become *Flash* **Seats** customers.

The *Flash* **Seats** system has the capability to be scaled at very little cost. For each venue using the system, traditional paper tickets will be gradually replaced by paperless tickets to be used in conjunction with the *Flash* **Seats** marketplace. Few additional costs will be incurred as the number of paperless tickets increases.

Initial sales forecasts for Year 2 and Year 3 will be eclipsed by Year 4 sales, at which point the first customer (e.g., venue) converts its entire ticketing operations to *Flash* **Seats**. As a result, Flash Seats Corp. will see a major growth in revenue in Year 4. This upward trend will continue into the future as more venues convert to the exclusive use of paperless tickets.

* Additional financial information given in Appendix C.

8.1. IMPORTANT ASSUMPTIONS

Before presenting the particulars of the financial data, this section identifies the major assumptions on which the figures are based.

Trading commission revenue is generated as per the revenue metrics below.

This section presents the hypothesis pertaining to one MLB team. However, all the figures closely resemble the figures for other sports teams (venues).

TICKET TRADING

For every game, 17 percent of all season ticket holders do not attend the event and currently do not trade their tickets because they do not have a medium to do so. Of this figure, 50 percent would trade their tickets if **Flash** Seats were in operation and they could use it.

At the same time, for every game, 25 percent of all season ticket holders do not attend and currently trade their tickets on the secondary market. All of these holders would switch to **Flash** Seats if this virtual marketplace were in operation and they could use it. Similarly, 25 percent of all non-season ticket holders do not attend and currently trade their tickets on the secondary market. All of these nonseason ticket holders would switch to **Flash** Seats if this system were in operation and they could use it.

In conclusion, **Flash** Seats provides a medium for ticket trading for both categories of ticket holders:

- People who would not trade their tickets if **Flash** Seats did not exist;
- People who currently trade their tickets on the secondary market.

TICKET PRICING

Average Ticket Face Value..$35.00
Average Percentage Increase over Face Value
(when ticket is traded on the Secondary Market)..........................40%
Average Price of Ticket Traded on Secondary Market................$49.00

There are three sources of revenue for Flash Seats Corp., as explained in section 2.0 and below.

TRADE COMMISSION

Revenues for both the venue and for Flash Seats Corp. are created by charging a commission for every transaction involving the exchange of a ticket. More precisely, a commission is perceived as a percentage of the trading price of every ticket. Thus, revenues are generated both when tickets trade at increasing prices as well as when they trade at decreasing values.

Commission buyer pays 10%
Commission seller pays 10%
Revenue created is divided as follows:
Flash Seats Corp 75%
Venue 25%

LICENSING FEE

Software licensing is $300,000 for a full venue installation, prorated for fewer seats. A fee is calculated based on the ratio of paperless tickets to total tickets.

MAINTENANCE FEE

Software maintenance is $10,000 for a full venue installation, prorated for fewer seats. A fee is calculated based on the ratio of paperless tickets to total tickets.

OTHER ASSUMPTIONS

Playoffs are not included in the calculations for potential revenue.

Potential revenues from full system deployment are as follows:
1 MLB team represents potentially.........................$ 6.2 million in revenue per season
1 NBA team represents potentially.........................$ 1.5 million in revenue per season
1 NHL team represents potentially.........................$ 1.2 million in revenue per season
1 NFL team represents potentially.........................$ 1.8 million in revenue per season

8.2. START-UP SUMMARY

The table that follows details the expenses related to the commencement of operations to develop and market *Flash* **Seats**. First, there are several typical expenses needed for the start-up of every company, such as legal expenses, office supplies, insurance, and logo artwork. Second, there are expenses related to the development of the software system itself. More specifically, these include:

- Web site design refers to the virtual environment in which the controlled exchange of tickets will occur.
- Development of the integrated system and buildout of application programming interface (API) refer to the creation of the virtual marketplace.
- Technical architecture design refers to the process of combining the technologies that form the *Flash* **Seats** system.
- Development of demo software refers to the beta-version of the *Flash* **Seats** marketplace that will be used before large-scale marketing operations begin;
- Expensed equipment includes all equipment needed by the Flash Seats Corp. (e.g., computers, printers, telephones).

Third, the table includes expenses regarding marketing materials. These are considered start-up costs because the marketing efforts will be coordinated with the system development operations. This aspect was fully explained in section 4.3 of the plan.

Flash Seats Corp. is seeking $1.2 million in start-up capital from investors, to fund the first year of development costs.

Exact figures follow in the table on the next page.

Start-up	
Requirements	
Start-up Expenses	
Legal Reserve	$25,000
Office Supplies	$250
Marketing Material	$15,000
Web Site Design	$65,000
Insurance	$500
Computers	$6,000
T&E	$3,000
Logo Artwork	$2,800
Create Working Demo	$4,500
Cell Phones	$1,000
Technical Architecture Design	$10,000
Development of Exchange	$100,000

continued

Start-up	
Buildout of APIs	$150,000
Beta Testing	$75,000
Build out at venues	$150,000
Other	$500
Total Start-up Expenses	**$608,550**
Start-up Assets Needed	
Cash Balance on Starting Date	$591,450
Total Current Assets	**$591,450**
Long-term Assets	$0
Total Assets	$591,450
Total Requirements	**$1,200,000**
Funding	
Investment	
Investor	$1,200,000
Total Investment	**$1,200,000**
Current Liabilities	$0
Long-term Liabilities	$0
Total Liabilities	$0
Loss at Start-up	($608,550)
Total Capital	$591,450
Total Capital and Liabilities	**$591,450**

8.3. BREAK-EVEN ANALYSIS

The current section presents the break-even analysis for *Flash* Seats.

Before presenting the figures, this part of the study defines the break-even scenario:

■ One implied customer: 1 MLB team;
■ All assumptions described in section 8.1 are taken into account.

Revenue... $ 161.49 per paperless ticket per season
Variable Cost per Seat................................. $ 24.22 (money transfer fees, etc.)
Fixed Cost for whole year........................... $ 513,000.00 (labor costs, etc.)
Number of paperless tickets
to break even... *3,737 seats (tickets)*

This break-even number of seats will be attained halfway through the second year.

8.4. PROJECTED PROFIT AND LOSS

The current section presents the financial data pertaining to projected profit and loss for *Flash* **Seats**.

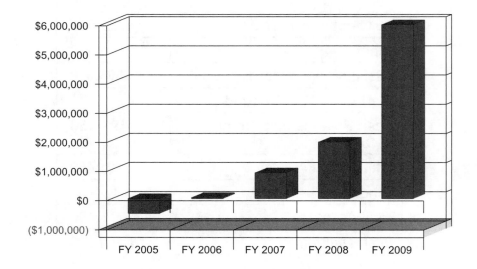

The graph shows profits for the first five years of operations. There is a loss of $500,000 during the first year due to expenses associated with the development of the system. During the second year there is a small positive cash flow, generated by the gradual deployment of venue seats. Throughout Year 3 and Year 4, net profits rise to $0.9 million and $2 million, respectively. In Year 5, the first MLB team customer becomes fully integrated into the *Flash* **Seats** system and this causes the large growth in revenue from the periods before. Profit in Year 5 is $6 million.

ENDNOTES
[1] www.ticketmaster.com. (January 2004).

[2] "TM to Launch Ticket Auction." www.Pollstar.com (September 2003).

[3] "Arts, Entertainment, and Recreation." *U.S. Census Bureau. Statistical Abstract of the United States 2002.*

[4] "Third-Party Ticketing Services, 2003." *The Houston Chronicle.* January 2003, p. 4.

[5] Idem 2.

[6] www.paciolan.com. January 2004.

[7] Idem 6.

[8] www.ustba.com. January 2004.

[9] www.onlinetickets.com. January 2004.

[10] Beltran, Eamon. "Amer Airlines E-Tickets." Dow Jones Newswires. May 1, 2003.

[11] www.truequote.com. January 2004.

[12] www.ebay.com. January 2004.

[13] Lewis, Peter. "Judge Tosses Ticket-Scalping Cases, cites M's Internet Sales." *Seattle Times.* January 31, 2004. http://seattletimes.nwsource.com/html/localnews/2001848018_mariners310.html. January 2004.

APPENDIX A *FLASH* SEATS FUNCTIONAL DIAGRAM

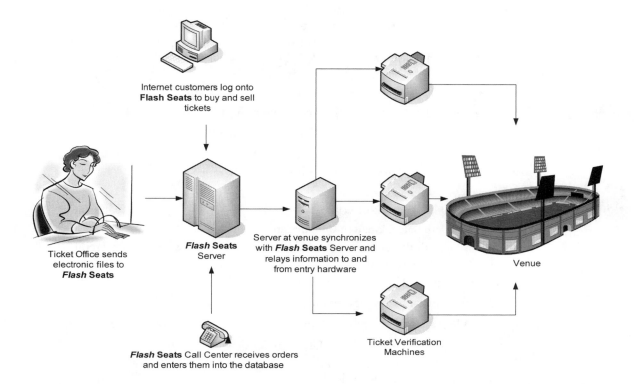

Internet customers log onto **Flash Seats** to buy and sell tickets

Ticket Office sends electronic files to **Flash Seats**

***Flash* Seats** Server

Server at venue synchronizes with **Flash Seats** Server and relays information to and from entry hardware

Venue

Ticket Verification Machines

***Flash* Seats** Call Center receives orders and enters them into the database

APPENDIX B   MANAGEMENT TEAM RESUMES

72 Flashseat ave   (760) 555.5555
Carlsbad, CA 92009   bnakfoor@flashseats.com

Brett A. Nakfoor

Education

Wharton School, University of Pennsylvania, Philadelphia, PA

B.S. Economics, Finance Major, History Minor, June 1991

Varsity Football, Sigma Chi Fraternity, Friars Senior Society

Experience

2002–2004 Money Network   Carlsbad, CA

Vice-President Sales, Western United States

In charge of all direct and channel sales in Western United States for credit and debit pay card vendor.

Manage team and channel reps.

Led company sales 2 years running.

Closed largest deals in company history in successive quarters of '03 & '04.

Responsible for P&L, sales strategy and strategic direction.

1998-2002 i2 Technologies   Chicago, IL

Account Executive

Sold Enterprise wide Supply Chain Mgmt and e-Business software applications.

Exceeded Quota each year at i2.

Salesman of the Year, 1999, 600% of quota.

Closed largest deal in company history for geographic region

Average Deal Size in excess of $2 MM.

Sold over $25 MM of software in 4 years.

Generated service sales in excess of $35 MM.

1991-1998 Chicago Mercantile Exchange   Chicago, IL

Independent Floor Trader

Traded futures in the pits of the Chicago Mercantile Exchange, the world's 2nd largest futures exchange.

Traded LIBOR, Eurodollar, S&P and Foreign Currency futures and options.

Chairman of the LIBOR pit.

Utilized various spreading strategies and options strategies.

Served on various governance committees.

Actively traded GLOBEX, CME's electronic trading system.

Interests

Sports, Entertainment, On-line Trading, Internet, History, Food & Wine

Sarah Coffman

33 Flashseat • Notre Dame, IN 46556 • 808.555.5555 • scoffman@flashseat.edu

Education

University of Notre Dame Graduate School of Business   Notre Dame, IN
Masters of Business Administration, May, 2005
- GMAT 720 (97 percentile overall)
- Full-tuition fellowship
- VP of Entrepreneur and Women in Business clubs, Co-Chair Community Service Committee

Brigham Young University   Provo, UT
Recreation Management and Youth Leadership
- Minors: Business Management
                 Ballroom Dance
- Graduated *cum laude*, member of Golden Key National Honor Society, academic scholarship

Work Experience

1990-2003   Coffman Concessions, Inc.   Wabash, IN
Vice President
- Converted least productive site in Miami, Florida into second most profitable
- Currently designing company website
- Maintained relationships and finances with fair directors, site managers, and suppliers
- Supervised staff, hired and trained new employees, led customer service, and oversaw food preparation for concessions

2002-2003   Leavitt Ready Mix   Moapa, NV
Construction Assistant
- Calculated and measured depth for over 3000 feet of underground pipes
- Directed machine operators and checked quality of assembly and installation of valve systems

2001   Glendale Elementary School   Glendale, AZ
Teacher
- Prepared and taught lessons in four core sixth-grade subjects at an inner city school
- Initiated and maintained communication with parents of thirty students

2000-2001   Anasazi Foundation   Mesa, AZ
Psychiatric Technician
- Promoted to supervisor during second week of work
- Learned and applied Arbinger principles of work, treatment, and relationships
- Researched success of program and significance of parent participation to help achieve better results

Activities

School Organizations: Studied abroad in Jerusalem and Columbia, performed with BYU ballroom dance team, started and directed BYU swing dance team, participated in campus service club
Volunteer experience: LDS Church, Big Brothers/Big Sisters, Community League soccer coach, Special Olympics, Sub for Santa and volunteer tutor
Part-time Employment: Glendale Community College, *Teacher*; Mesa Public School System, *Substitute*; Lone Eagle Resort, *Intern*; Three Rivers Ballroom Dance Company, *Intern*

100 Flashseat
Notre Dame, IN 46556

(574) 555-5555
jfrancis@flashseat.edu

Joshua Francis

Education

Masters of Business Administration, University of Notre Dame, Notre Dame, IN, 2005
- Part Tuition Fellowship
- Business and Technology Club
- McCloskey Business Plan Semi Finalist

Bachelors of Science, Applied Physics, Brigham Young University, Provo, UT, 2003
- Chemistry Emphasis
- Mathematics Minor

Work Experience

2003   **Continental Tire**   Hanover, Germany
Consultant
- Assisted Professor Jim Davis in training mid level management in Corporate Strategy
- Assisted Management Groups in corporate projects designed by senior management

2000–Present   **Center for Instructional**   DesignProvo, UT
Research Assistant
- Restructured media objects to save over $70,000 in production costs
- Managed team of faculty and students developing physics independent study courses
- Maintained web-based database for course elements
- Wrote, formatted, and edited course text and designed computer animations allowing the students a hands on feel to the online labs used
- Scripted, filmed, and edited video portions of labs

1997-2003   **Discount Fireworks**   Bozeman, MT
Manager
- Co-manager of a chain of fireworks stands
- Directed marketing, logistics, and personnel for chain adapting to specific selling needs
- Doubled the number of stands and experienced a 300% growth in profits

1998-2000 **The Church of Jesus Christ of Latter-Day Saints**   Sao Paulo, Brazil
Volunteer Service Representative
- Directed service efforts in three cities
- Fluent in Portuguese
- Familiar with Culture and Lifestyle of Brazil

Interests: Team 2002 Olympic Volunteer, Eagle Scout - Boy Scouts of America, Society of Physics Students, Amateur Films, Athletics

Computer Skills: Maple and Matlab (3 years), Java, Pascal, Visual Basic, LabView, Microsoft Office Products, PC and Macintosh OS, Kaleidagraph, Solidworks, Photoshop, Adobe Premier, DreamWeaver, Networking (Wi-Fi and Ethernet).

Justin Carter

100 Flashseat Place • Notre Dame • Indiana • 46556 • (574) 555-5555 • jcarter5@flashseat.com

Education

2003 – 2005   **MASTERS OF BUSINESS ADMININSTRATION**
University of Notre Dame, Notre Dame, IN, USA

1996 – 2000   **BACHELOR OF MECHANICAL ENGINEERING**
Concentration in Computer-Integrated Manufacturing
Carleton University, Ottawa, ON, Canada

Experience

Operations Manager 2002 – 2003 Bank & Vogue Ltd.

- Brokered wholesale commodities (textiles and electronics) in the international market.
- Facilitated logistical planning of daily export operations including all documentation requirements for international trade to South America, Africa, Europe and Asia.
- Re-engineered daily operations by implementing and designing a database tracking system for the export of wholesale commodities, that increased transaction processing rates and the tracking capabilities of each shipment.
- Analyzed profitability of a joint business venture with a local charity that resulted in the implementation of a mutually beneficial business partnership.

Supply Chain Management 2001 – 2003 Salaama Computers Ltd.

- Managed export operations of wholesale electronics to Africa.
- Created and managed supply chain of wholesale electronic suppliers for international export.
- Consolidated and inspected shipments before exporting goods.

Mechanical Design 2000 – 2001 JDS Uniphase

- Designed two rack mountable fiberoptic switches. Responsible for complete sheet metal chassis design and integration of fiberoptic and electronic components. Created Printed Circuit Board common feature layout (connector / button positions, keep-outs, etc.).
- Supported existing manufacturing processes including re-design of products and procedures, resulting in higher quality products, produced at a more efficient rate.
- Created product structures and bill of materials for existing and new products streamlining process to allow a faster turn around time from customer order to product shipment date.

Formula SAE Team Captain 1998 – 2000 Carleton University

- Led the design and development of an open-wheel, open-cockpit racecar for a student competition held by the Society of Automotive Engineers (SAE) in Detroit Michigan (1998 – 2000).
- Managed and recruited a 75 member student race team (1998 – 2000).
- Received Dean Malcolm J. Bibby Thumbs-Up Award, granted for the most outstanding student project in engineering (1999).
- Received two Carleton Student Engineering Society Leadership Awards for "outstanding contributions to the betterment of engineering student life at Carleton University" (1999 & 2000).
- Awarded Mechanical & Aerospace Engineering H.I.H. Saravanamuttoo Scholarship for leadership role in FSAE project, granted on high academic standing and demonstrated leadership (2000).
- Created, managed and allocated project budget of $35,000 and $45,000 (1999 & 2000 respectively).

Interests

- Racecars, Computer Technology, Jogging, Football

UNIV. OF NOTRE DAME • APT 2C • 20 FISCHER GRADUATE RES. • NOTRE DAME, IN 46556
PHONE (574) 634-4411 • E-MAIL ROLIEVSC@ND.EDU

RADU A. OLIEVSCHI

EDUCATION

University of Notre Dame	Notre Dame, Indiana	2003-2005
Masters of Business Administration – Marketing, Human Resources		
Utica College of Syracuse University	Utica, New York	1999-2003
Bachelor of Science in International Management		
Performing Arts		

ACADEMIC RECORD AND AWARDS

- Full tuition fellowship – University of Notre Dame
- Top 2% GMAT Score (740 Total)
- Academic Affairs Committee
- Marketing Club

- Valedictorian – 2003 – Utica College of Syracuse University
- DiSpirito Award for Excellence in Art, 2003
- Dean Woods Student Life Award – contributions to quality of campus life, 2003

WORK EXPERIENCE

2002 – 2003 Utica College of Syracuse University Utica, NY	*Teaching and Research Assistant – French*	Taught classes and conducted conversation groups; contributed to evaluating students; provided help outside classes; conducted research for various projects (i.e. French authors, confidential book project by Dr. Marie-Noelle Little).
2001 – 2002 Walt Disney Company Orlando, FL	*Marketing Cast Member*	Sales and advertising representative; restocking operations; hosting theme park marketing locations.
2001 Utica College of Syracuse University Utica, NY	*Assistant in Office of International Admissions*	Contributed to establishing the Office of International Admissions. Duties included: processing mail, replying to inquiries, student database creation and updating; public relations activities. Full responsibilities during supervisor's absence.

LANGUAGES

Fluent in English, French, and Romanian.

EXTRACURRICULAR ACTIVITIES

Senator – Utica College of Syracuse University Student Senate, 1999-2000 • Vice President of Windows to the World – Utica College's International Student Club, 2002-2003 • Journalist for Utica College's newspaper *The Tangerine*, 2002-2003 • Chairperson on the Utica College Programming Board organizing entertainment events on campus, 2000.

COMMUNITY ACTIVITIES AND INTERESTS

Member of New Hartford Players Youth Theatre in Utica-Rome, New York, 1999-2001 • Directing jobs: multimedia show of Edward Albee's *Counting the Ways* (2003), selections of *Butterflies Are Free, California Suite*, etc. • Roles in college and regional productions: Louis in *Personals*, Arthur/others in *The Dinning Room*, Hamlet in *Fortinbras*, Tybalt in *Romeo and Juliet*, Dracula in *Dracula: The Musical?*, Landlord/Captain in *The Robber Bridegroom*, Bill/Trotksy in *All in the Timing* etc. • Author of numerous short stories, currently working on first novel • Trained as a film critic by ProCinema Magazine (biggest Romanian film publication), 1996-1999 • First place in scriptwriting competition by Atomic TV (Romanian MTV) for *Soul's Windows*, 1999.

APPENDIX C PRO FORMA PROFIT AND LOSS

Profit and Loss

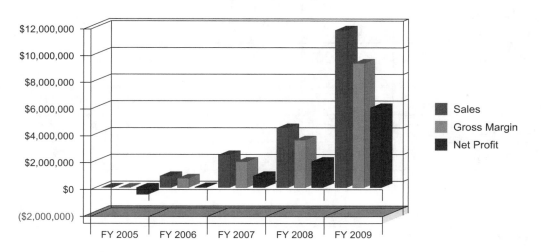

Pro Forma Profit and Loss					
	FY 2005	FY 2006	FY 2007	FY 2008	FY 2009
Sales (in dollars)	0	870,422	2,433,891	4,462,483	11,785,502
Direct Cost of Sales (in dollars)	0	179,432	502,409	924,074	2,485,131
	------------	------------	------------	------------	------------
Total Cost of Sales (in dollars)	0	179,432	502,409	924,074	2,485,131
Gross Margin (in dollars)	0	690,990	1,931,481	3,538,409	9,300,371
Gross Margin (%)	0	79.39	79.36	79.29	78.91
Expenses:					
Payroll (in dollars)	300,000	408,000	408,000	468,000	468,000
Office Suppliers (in dollars)	3,000	3,000	4,000	5,000	6,000
Cell Phone (in dollars)	12,000	12,000	15,000	15,000	17,000
T&E (in dollars)	36,000	36,000	40,000	45,000	50,000
Health Care/Benefits (in dollars)	27,000	27,000	30,000	35,000	40,000
Legal (in dollars)	24,000	24,000	24,000	24,000	24,000
Hosting (in dollars)	60,000	60,000	80,000	90,000	100,000

continued

Payroll Taxes (in dollars)	45,000	61,200	61,200	70,200	70,200
Other (in dollars)	6,000	6,000	7,000	7,000	7,000
Total Operating Expenses (in dollars)	513,000	637,200	669,200	759,200	782,200
Profit Before Interest and Taxes (in dollars)	(513,000)	53,790	1,262,281	2,779,209	8,518,171
Taxes Incurred (in dollars)	0	16,137	378,684	833,763	2,555,451
Net Profit (in dollars)	(513,000)	37,653	883,597	1,945,446	5,962,720
Net Profit/Sales (%)	0	4.33	36.30	43.60	50.59

APPENDIX D   PROJECTED STATEMENT OF CASH FLOWS

The table below presents the projected Statement of Cash Flows for *Flash* Seats.

Pro Forma Cash Flow					
	FY 2005	FY 2006	FY 2007	FY 2008	FY 2009
Cash Received					
Cash from Operations:					
Cash Sales (in dollars)	0	870,422	2,433,891	4,462,483	11,785,502
Cash from Receivables (in dollars)	0	0	0	0	0
Subtotal Cash from Operations (in dollars)	0	870,422	2,433,891	4,462,483	11,785,502
Expenditures	FY 2005	FY 2006	FY 2007	FY 2008	FY 2009
Expenditures from Operations:					
Cash Spending (in dollars)	300,000	408,000	408,000	468,000	468,000
Payment of Accounts Payable (in dollars)	195,250	400,429	1,066,691	1,950,943	5,000,672
Subtotal Spent on Operations (in dollars)	495,250	808,429	1,474,691	2,418,943	5,468,672
Net Cash Flow (in dollars)	(495,250)	61,993	959,200	2,043,541	6,316,830
Cash Balance (in dollars)	96,200	158,193	1,117,393	3,160,934	9,477,764

The table below presents the projected Statement of Cash Flows for Year 2 for *Flash* Seats.

Pro Forma Cash Flow Year 2	Apr	May	Jun	Jul	Aug	Sep	Oct	Nov	Dec	Jan	Feb	Mar
Cash Received												
Cash from Operations:												
Cash Sales (in dollars)	43,913	43,913	43,913	43,913	83,787	83,787	127,740	127,740	47,992	47,992	87,866	87,866
Cash from Receivables (in dollars)	0	0	0	0	0	0	0	0	0	0	0	0
Subtotal Cash from Operations (in dollars)	43,913	43,913	43,913	43,913	83,787	83,787	127,740	127,740	47,992	47,992	87,866	87,866
Expenditures	Apr	May	Jun	Jul	Aug	Sep	Oct	Nov	Dec	Jan	Feb	Mar
Expenditures from Operations:												
Cash Spending (in dollars)	34,000	34,000	34,000	34,000	34,000	34,000	34,000	34,000	34,000	34,000	34,000	34,000
Payment of Accounts Payable (in dollars)	17,750	22,624	22,624	22,624	22,624	40,866	40,866	60,332	60,332	23,848	23,848	42,090
Subtotal Spent on Operations (in dollars)	51,750	56,624	56,624	56,624	56,624	74,866	74,866	94,332	94,332	57,848	57,848	76,090
Net Cash Flow (in dollars)	(7,837)	(12,711)	(12,711)	(12,711)	27,163	8,921	52,873	33,407	(46,340)	(9,856)	30,018	11,776
Cash Balance (in dollars)	88,363	75,652	62,942	50,231	77,394	86,314	139,188	172,595	126,255	116,399	146,417	158,193

Cash Second Year

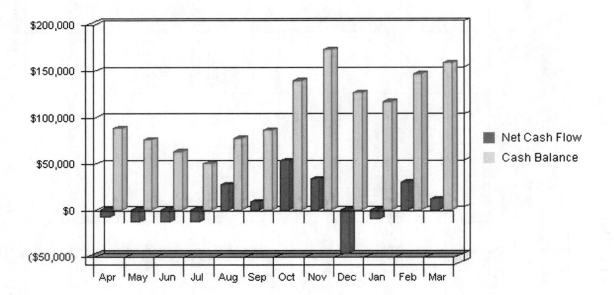

APPENDIX F   SALES FORECAST FOR YEAR 2

The table below presents the Sales Forecast for Year 2 for *Flash* Seats.

Sales Forecast Year 2

Sales	Apr	May	Jun	Jul	Aug	Sep	Oct	Nov	Dec	Jan	Feb	Mar
Trading Commissions (in dollars)	39,874	39,874	39,874	39,874	79,748	79,748	119,621	119,621	39,874	39,874	79,748	79,748
Software Licenses (in dollars)	1,974	1,974	1,974	1,974	1,974	1,974	5,921	5,921	5,921	5,921	5,921	5,921
Software Maintenance (in dollars)	66	66	66	66	66	66	197	197	197	197	197	197
Advertising (in dollars)	2,000	2,000	2,000	2,000	2,000	2,000	2,000	2,000	2,000	2,000	2,000	2,000
Total Sales (in dollars)	43,913	43,913	43,913	43,913	83,787	83,787	127,740	127,740	47,992	47,992	87,866	87,866

Direct Cost of Sales	Apr	May	Jun	Jul	Aug	Sep	Oct	Nov	Dec	Jan	Feb	Mar
Money Transfer Fees (in dollars)	8,972	8,972	8,972	8,972	17,943	17,943	26,915	26,915	8,972	8,972	17,943	17,943
Subtotal Direct Cost of Sales (in dollars)	8,972	8,972	8,972	8,972	17,943	17,943	26,915	26,915	8,972	8,972	17,943	17,943

Sales Monthly Second Year

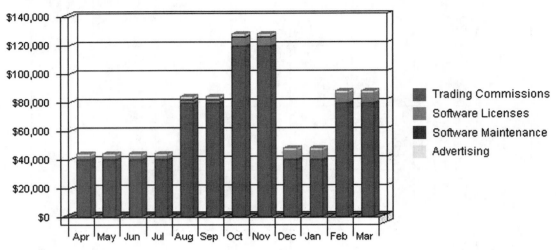

APPENDIX G   PROJECTED BALANCE SHEET

The table below presents the projected Balance Sheet for *Flash* Seats.

Pro Forma Balance Sheet					
Assets					
Current Assets	FY 2005	FY 2006	FY 2007	FY 2008	FY 2009
Cash (in dollars)	96,200	158,193	1,117,393	3,160,934	9,477,764
Total Current Assets (in dollars)	96,200	158,193	1,117,393	3,160,934	9,477,764
Long-term Assets (in dollars)	0	0	0	0	0
Total Assets (in dollars)	96,200	158,193	1,117,393	3,160,934	9,477,764
Liabilities and Capital					
Current Liabilities	FY 2005	FY 2006	FY 2007	FY 2008	FY 2009
Accounts Payable (in dollars)	17,750	42,090	117,693	215,787	569,898
Subtotal Current Liabilities (in dollars)	17,750	42,090	117,693	215,787	569,898
Long-term Liabilities (in dollars)	0	0	0	0	0

continued

Total Liabilities (in dollars)	17,750	42,090	117,693	215,787	569,898
Paid-in Capital (in dollars)	1,200,000	1,200,000	1,200,000	1,200,000	1,200,000
Retained Earnings (in dollars)	(608,550)	(1,121,550)	(1,083,897)	(200,300)	1,745,146
Earnings (in dollars)	(513,000)	37,653	883,597	1,945,446	5,962,720
Total Capital (in dollars)	78,450	116,103	999,700	2,945,146	8,907,866
Total Liabilities and Capital (in dollars)	96,200	158,193	1,117,393	3,160,934	9,477,764
Net Worth (in dollars)	78,450	116,103	999,700	2,945,146	8,907,866

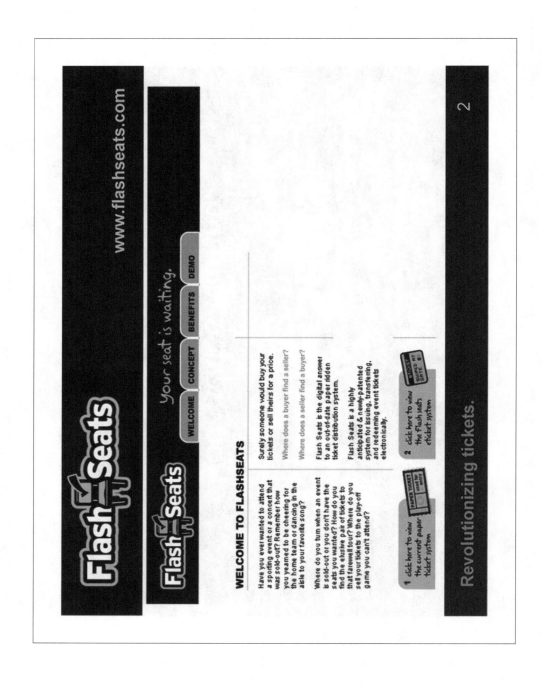

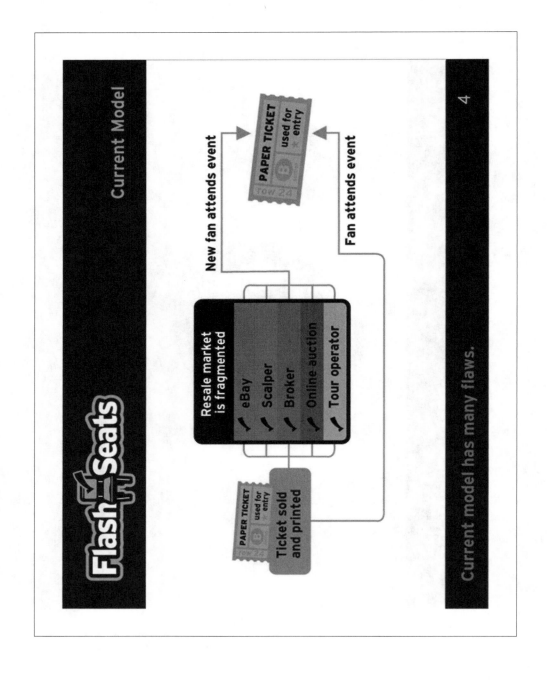

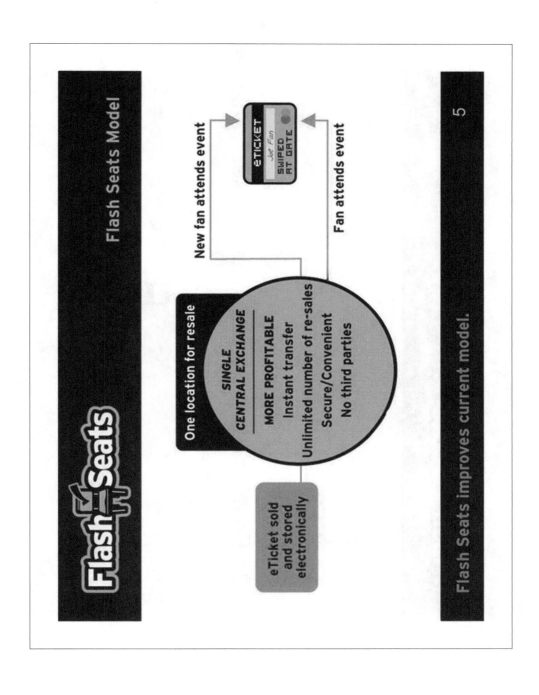

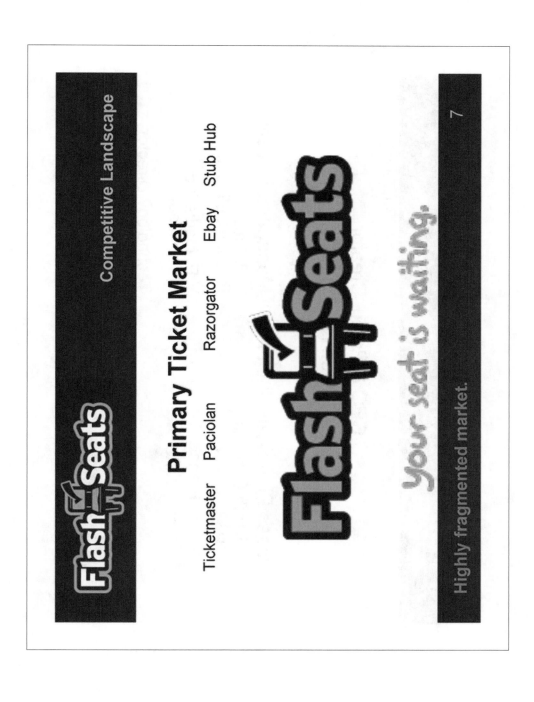

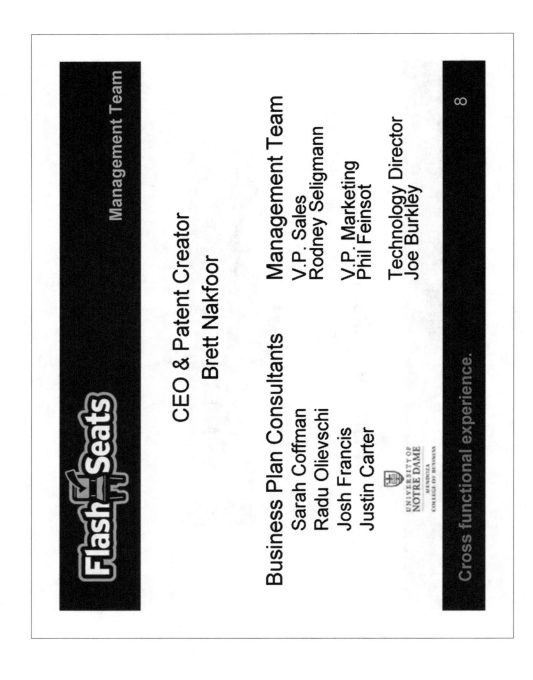

Revenue Model

Four Fundamentals:

1. Paper-less

2. Centralized exchange

3. Commission based revenue

4. $10 –14 Billion market size*

*Source: Jupiter Media Metrix 2001; Happel and Jennings Article, Cato Journal, Winter 2002

Revenue from each transaction.

9

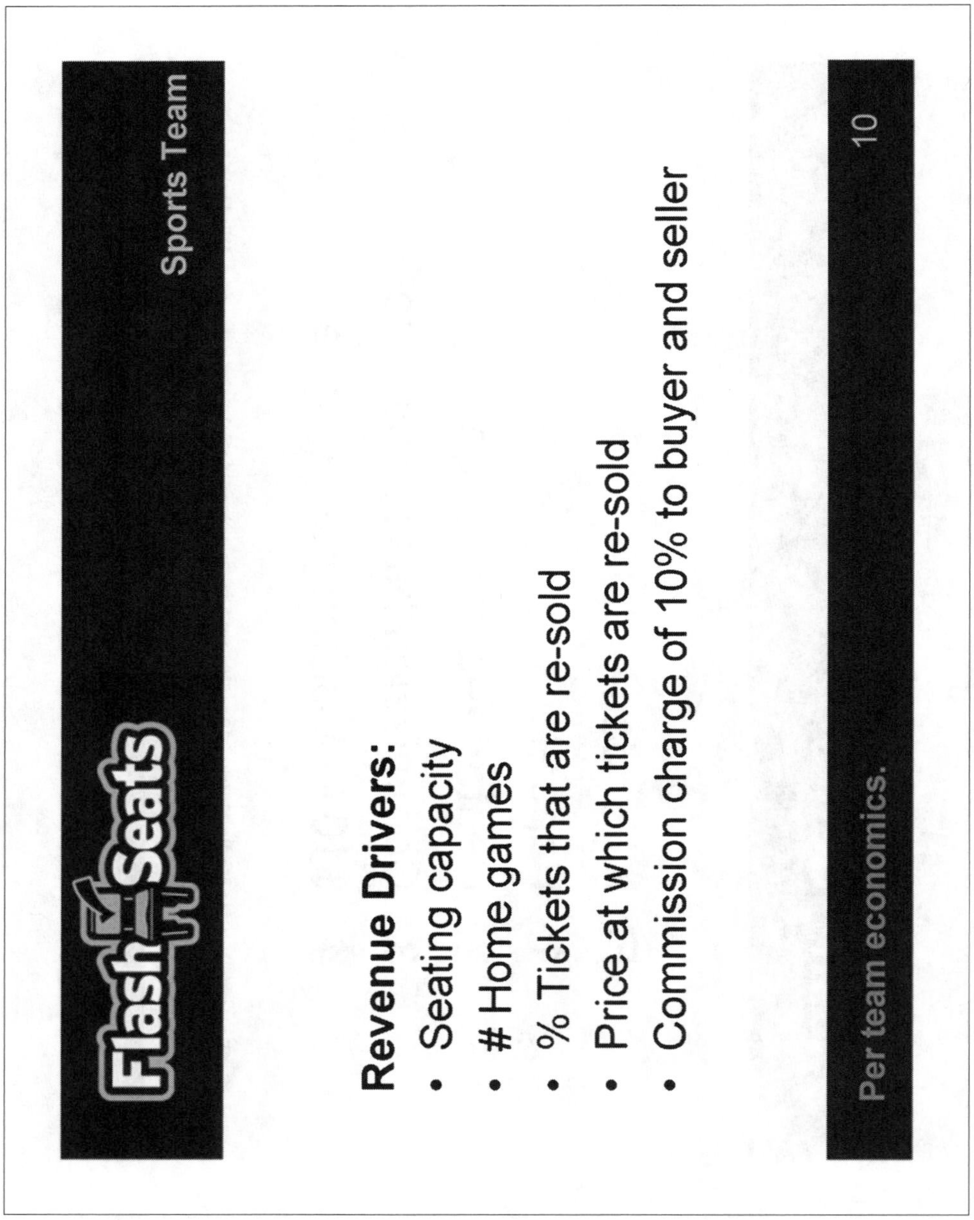
FlashSeats
Sports Team
Revenue Drivers:
• Seating capacity
• # Home games
• % Tickets that are re-sold
• Price at which tickets are re-sold
• Commission charge of 10% to buyer and seller
Per team economics.
10

Sports Team Economics

Gross Revenue Generated:

- MLB Team = $2.9 Million*
- NFL Team = $1.6 Million*
- NBA Team = $1.2 Million*

MLB Team Example:

81 Home Games X 45,000 Seats X 75% Capacity X 6% Resold X $30 Face Value

X 175% Price Increase X 20% Commission = $1,722,262 (regular season)

= $1,215,000 (playoffs)

= **$2.9 Million**

*Playoff Contending Team

Scaleable Revenues.

11

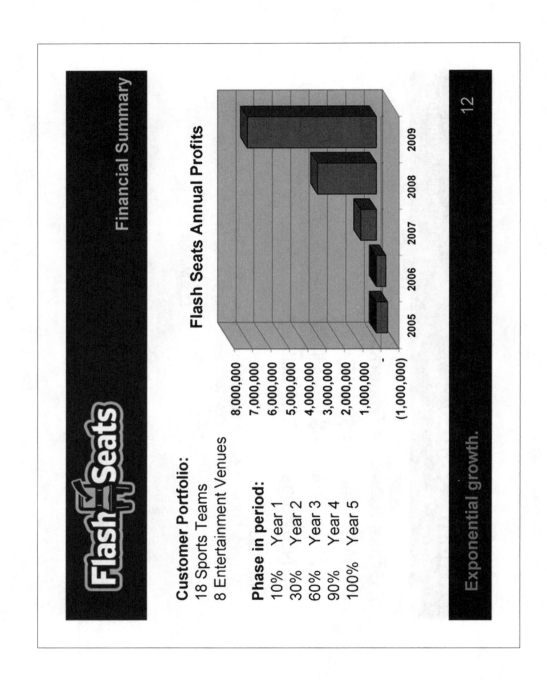

Flash Seats

Current Status

Achieved Milestones:
- Intellectual Property
- www.flashseats.com
- Online Demo
- Ongoing sales cycles
- Invested $60,000

Looking Foreword:
- Seeking Investment of $1.5 Million

Make the call.

13

Flash Seats

Exit Strategy

1. Competitor Buyout
   - Ticketmaster
   - Paciolan
   - Razorgator
   - Ebay
   - TimeWarner
   - Stub Hub
2. IPO

Everyone wins.

14

C BUSINESS PLAN COMPETITION RESOURCES

http://www.smallbusinessnotes.com/planning/competitions.html

There are a wide variety of business plan competitions held worldwide. Listed below are some of the better-known competitions. With new competitions being announced on a regular basis, maintaining a comprehensive list is challenging. To see if there is a competition near you, visit the **Web sites of business schools** located near you.

Asian MOOT Corp
Competition between the graduate business programs in Asia. The winner of the Moot Corp competition at the University of Texas represents the United States at this event.

Babson College Business Plan Competition
Separate undergraduate and graduate student events.

Bank One Business Competition
Participants must be students in the Business Plan Preparation Course at the University of Colorado–Boulder.

Bioscience Business Plan Competition
Open to academics, postdoctoral scientists, and PhD students in all UK universities and BBSRC-sponsored research institutes.

Burton D. Morgan Entrepreneurship Competition
All Purdue students are eligible to participate in the event. Nonstudents—such as students from other colleges, Purdue alumni, and local residents—can also be team members, but Purdue students must make the final presentations to the judges.

Case-Weatherhead Business Launch Competition
Participants must have a technology-based business concept, have at least one team member who is affiliated with Case Western Reserve University as a student, faculty member, or alumnus.

Ceem Business Plan Competition
Open to all currently registered University of California, Santa Barbara students.

CIBC Ivey Business Plan Competition
Open to teams of two to six MBA students enrolled in an accredited Canadian University.

The Duke Start-up Challenge
Each team must include one full-time student in any program at Duke.

E-Challenge
All Stanford students, research and postdoctoral staff, and faculty are eligible to enter the Stanford Entrepreneur's Challenge. Although individuals not affiliated with Stanford University are encouraged to participate, any entering team must have at least half of its members affiliated with Stanford University.

Eureka!
The B-Plan competition of Indian Institute of Technology, Bombay. At least one member of the team must be a student. Student can be of any college, any university.

First Capital Challenge
$50,000 competition for the best plan to start a high-potential business in Kingston, Ontario, Canada. Open to anyone, anywhere.

GSAS Harvard Biotechnology Club Business Plan Competition
Open to entrepreneurs, students, and professionals worldwide, and does not require Harvard University affiliation. The competition offers a $5,000 cash award for the first prize, a $1,000 cash award for second prize, and an opportunity for early stage biotechnology companies to have their business plans reviewed by seasoned venture capitalists focused on this industry and other biotechnology experts in the Boston area.

Global Social Venture Competition
Students must create business plans that demonstrate both economic and social value. Each team must have an actively involved, current MBA student from any business school in the United States or abroad.

Great Lakes Entrepreneur's Quest
Any person or group that has a business concept focused in or based on technology (such as an e-commerce platform, a life sciences application, or advanced manufacturing breakthrough) can compete in the business plan competition. Each team must include at least one member who resides, works, or attends school in Michigan.

Harvard Business School Business Plan Competition
Every team must have a minimum of one Harvard Business School second year student.

The Marriott School Business Plan Competition
Open to Brigham Young University students.

Maximum Exposure Business Plan Competition
Participating teams must consist of at least one current New York University Leonard N. Stern School of Business MBA student. The competition is also known as the Stern $50K Plus.

Melbourne University Entrepreneurs' Challenge
Open to all members of the Melbourne University community. One team member must be a student of the university.

The MIT $50K Entrepreneurship Competition
All full-time and part-time MIT students at all levels of education and from any department, registered with MIT for the current semester, are eligible to enter.

The Moot Corp Competition
One of the original competitions. MBAs from business schools around the globe come to the University of Texas at Austin each year to present their business plans to panels of investors.

New Venture Challenge
Each team is required to have at least one student from the Graduate School of Business, University of Chicago. This includes campus, part-time, evening, or weekend students.

New Venture Champion
Interuniversity competition sponsored by the University of Oregon.

Oxford University Business Plan Competition
Open to anyone with an imaginative idea for creating a new business. Located in Oxford, England, UK.

Palo Alto Software Business Planning Competition
Contestants must submit plans that are for a new business that has been running less than one year, or for an expansion of an existing business. All plans must be in Business Plan Pro format.

Rice University Business Plan Competition
Hosted by the Rice Alliance for Technology and Entrepreneurship, the Rice University Business Plan competition is open to graduate student teams from all universities who are interested in funding their company.

Syracuse Business Plan Competition
Open to all graduate and undergraduate students enrolled at Syracuse University. Students must have been enrolled during at least one semester of the current academic year. Over $40,000 in prizes awarded to top three teams. Help sessions available to teams through the Business Plan Laboratory. Intents to compete can be submitted online.

Tech Valley Collegiate Business Plan Competition
Open to all full-time registered students in a college or university located within the 19-county Tech Valley region. Cash and prizes total $50K.

The SkiView Business Plans Competition
An in-house competition for students from the University of Arizona enrolled in the Berger Entrepreneurship Program.

UC Berkeley Business Plan Competition
A self-funded, student-run competition open to ventures run by UC Berkeley students and alumni.

UMass Lowell $10K Business Plan Competition
Open to all current UML registered students and alumni within one year of their graduation.

University of San Francisco International Business Plan Competition
The competition is open to graduate students from all universities and features a Judging Panel of Silicon Valley Venture Capitalists and $25,000 in cash prizes.

University of Washington Business Plan Competition
Open to students who are enrolled in degree-seeking programs at Washington State University, Seattle Pacific University, Pacific Lutheran University, Seattle University, and the University of Washington.

V. Dale Cozad Business Plan Contest
Open to all persons 18 years and older. Additionally, at least one member of each team must be a full-time student of the University of Illinois at Urbana-Champaign and be in good standing during the duration of the competition.

Venture Adventure
An undergraduate business plan competition hosted by the Center for Entrepreneurial & Family Enterprises at Colorado State University.

Venture Challenge
San Diego State University Business Plan Competition, open to all students enrolled currently or during the calendar year prior to the competition.

Wharton Business Plan Competition
Any student(s) in any School of the University of Pennsylvania are eligible to participate as individuals or on teams. At least one member of each team must be an active student at the University of Pennsylvania (graduate or undergraduate). Partnerships between students and nonstudents are eligible.

WPI Venture Forum Business Plan Contest
To be eligible, Business Plans must involve technology-based ventures and describe the development of a new product, a new application or process in an existing business, or the start-up of a new business.

Y50K Yale Entrepreneurship Competition
A university-wide business plan competition that provides start-up funding as well as educational, networking, and mentoring opportunities to Yale entrepreneurs.

MOOT CORP COMPETITIONS

Participation in the Moot Corp Competition is through invitation or by winning one of the participating competitions. Winners from the following competitions are invited to participate in the Moot Corp Competition. The dates and contact information for these participating competitions are listed on their Web site, http://www.mootcorp.org/competitions.asp

Idea to Product Competition
http://www.ideatoproduct.org
Hosted by The University of Texas at Austin
Contact info@ideatoproduct.org

The John Heine Entrepreneurial Challenge
http://www.johnheinechallenge.org
Hosted by the Brisbane Graduate School of Business
Queensland University of Technology, Australia
Contact Belinda Hopgood at b.hopgood@qut.edu.au or 61 07 3138 4029.

Georgia Bowl
Hosted by Kennesaw State University
Contact Charles Hofer at 770-455-4555 or jrmh@bellsouth.net

Cardinal Challenge
http://www.cardinalchallenge.com
Hosted by the University of Louisville
Contact Van G.H. Clouse at 502-852-6440 or clouse@louisville.edu

UC Spirit of Enterprise MBA Business Plan Competition
http:///www.ecenter.uc.edu
Hosted by the University of Cincinnati
Contact Charles Matthews at 513-556-7123 or ecenter@uc.edu

FGV Latin Moot Corp Competition
http://latinmootcorp.fgv.br
Hosted by Fundacao Getulio Vargas, Sao Paulo, Brazil
Contact Laura Cristina Pansarella at cenn@fgvsp.br or Rene Jose Rodrigues Fernandes at rene.rodrigues@fgvsp.br

Northwest Venture Championship
http://www.northwestventurechampionship.org
Hosted by Boise State University
Contact Kent E. Neupert at 208-426-2397 or kneupert@boisestate.edu

Camino Real Venture Competition
http://caminorealcompetition.org
Hosted by University of Texas at El Paso
Contact Nancy Lowery at 915.534.8121 or nlowery@bnsl.org.

Thammasat Asia Moot Corp® Competition
http://www.asiamootcorp.org
Hosted by Thammasat University, Thailand
Contact Bill Randall at 662-652-6237 or info@asiamootcorp.org.

McGinnis Venture Competition
http://www.mcginnisventurecompetition.com
Hosted by Carnegie Mellon University
Contact Art Boni at 412-268-8685 or boni@andrew.cmu.edu

CEDIC New Venture Championship
http://www.big12cedic.com
Hosted by the Center for Economic Development, Innovation and Commercialization
Contact Gary Cadenhead at cadenheadg@mail.utexas.edu

Venture Challenge
http://www-rohan.sdsu.edu/dept/emc/pageVentureChallenge.shtml
Hosted by the Entrepreneurial Management Center
San Diego State University
Contact Sarah Bonura at 619-594-2781 or sbonura@projects.sdsu.edu

IBK Capital Ivey Business Plan Competition
http://www.iveybpc.com
Hosted by the Richard Ivey School of Business
University of Western Ontario
Contact Eric Morse at 519-661-4220 or emorse@ivey.uwo.ca or Sarah Buck at sbuck@ivey.ca

Wake Forest Elevator Competition
http://www.mba.wfu.edu/elevator
Hosted by Wake Forest University
Contact Donna Fulp at 336-758-5103 or Donna.Fulp@mba.wfu.edu

Lunar Ventures
http://www.8clunarventures.com
Hosted by Colorado School of Mines
Contact Gary Cadenhead at info@8clunarventures.com

USF-PSI International Business Plan Competition
http://www.usfca.edu/sobam/nvc
Hosted by the University of San Francisco
Contact Mark Cannice at 415-422-6785 or cannice@usfca.edu

Rice University Business Plan Competition
http://www.alliance.rice.edu/rbpc
Hosted by the Rice Alliance for Technology and Entrepreneurship Rice University
Contact Brad Burke at 713-348-6354 or rbpc@rice.edu

Stuart Clark Venture Challenge
http://www.stuartclark.org
Hosted by the Asper Centre for Entrepreneurship
University of Manitoba
Contact Rob Warren at 204-474-8422 or Robert_Warren@umanitoba.ca

Utah Entrepreneur Challenge
http://uechallenge.business.utah.edu
Hosted by University of Utah
Contact Leonard Black at 801-585-5575 or Leonard.Black@business.utah.edu

New Ventures World Competition
http://www.cba.unl.edu/outreach/ent/bpc
Hosted by the Nebraska Center for Entrepreneurship
University of Nebraska-Lincoln
Contact Glenn Friendt at 402-472-3353 or friendt2@unl.edu or entprenshp@unlnotes.unl.edu

New Venture Championship
http://www.venturechampionship.com
Hosted by the Lundquist Center for Entrepreneurship
University of Oregon
Contact Marianne Rosen-Murr at 541-346-3420 or mtmurr@uoregon.edu

Uniandes Moot Corp Business Plan Competition
http://mootcorp.uniandes.edu.co
Hosted by Universidad de los Andes, Colombia
Contact Rafael Vesga at 541-346-3420 or rav@adm.uniandes.edu.co

OFC Venture Challenge
http://www.ofcvc.org
Hosted by Clark Atlanta University
Contact Mohammad Bhuiyan at 404-880-8657 or ofcvc@hotmail.com

INDEX